CREATING A HEALTHY LIFE AND MARRIAGE

Blessings to you on your journey.

Judith Anne Desjardins

CREATING A HEALTHY LIFE AND MARRIAGE

Judith Anne Desjardins,
LCSW, BCD, MSWAC

Spirit House Publishing

CREATING A HEALTHY LIFE AND MARRIAGE
Judith Anne Desjardins

Published by: Spirit House Publishing
Address: 3435 Ocean Park Blvd., #107-418
           Santa Monica, CA 90405
           Telephone: 310-701-5481
           Fax: 310-392-6281
           Website: www.SpiritHousePub.com
           E-mail: SpiritHousePub@verizon.net

ISBN: 978-0-9843875-0-2

Library of Congress Control Number: 2009913505

First Edition. Printed in the United States of America
10 9 8 7 6 5 4 3 2 1

Direct Passages from Erik H. Erikson's *Childhood and Society*. Copyright 1950, © 1963 by W. W. Norton & Company, Inc., renewed © 1978, 1991 by Erik H. Erikson. Used by permission of W.W. Norton & Company, Inc. Published in the UK by the Hogarth Press. Reprinted by permission of The Random House Group Ltd.

Direct Passages reprinted with permission from the *Diagnostic and Statistical Manual of Mental Disorders, Text Revision, Fourth Edition* (Copyright 2000). American Psychiatric Association.

Cover and Page Design by One-On-One Book Production, West Hills, California.

Disclaimer

The purpose of this book is to educate you about your *"Self"* and your relationships. This book is not intended to take the place of psychotherapy or other appropriate health care. Readers are strongly urged to consult an appropriate health care professional to determine if treatment is necessary.

Dedication

*To my husband, children, grandchildren
and my Inner Children.
Thank you for the opportunity to love,
to learn, to grow and to transform.*

ACKNOWLEDGMENTS

This book has been germinating inside me for fifteen years and has been written in stages, according to the lessons I have learned. Each chapter is the result of my clinical and personal education and growth.

Because writing a book can be a rather daunting, grueling endeavor, I would like to take this opportunity to acknowledge those people, institutions and experiences which have helped me with the process.

I will begin by acknowledging the institutions and Social Service staffs which provided my clinical training, excellent clinical supervision, and access to the patients and clients who taught me so much:

- In Phoenix, Arizona: Maricopa County General Hospital and Saint Joseph's Hospital and In-Patient Psychiatric Unit.
- In Santa Monica, California: Saint John's Hospital and Oncology Unit and Ocean Park Community Center's Turning Point Homeless Shelter.
- In Venice, California: Didi Hirsch Community Mental Health and OutPatient Substance Abuse Services.

Next, I would like to acknowledge my training and studies in Los Angeles, California, at the following institutes:

- The Gestalt Therapy Institute, the Jin Shin Do Acupressure Foundation, and the C. G. Jung Institute and Library

Finally, I would like to thank the following:

- my private practice clients who gave me permission to use their material and testimonials.
- Pia Mellody and her work with codependency. Her book, *Facing Codependence; What It Is, Where It Comes From, How It Sabotages Our Lives,* has been invaluable on my journey and is the best definitive work on the subject. I have applied these principles to my own life and to the lives of my clients, and we have been greatly blessed.
- *Steps For Recovery* newspaper and Glenn Major, founder and editor of AnonymousOne.com — a Website for recovery, serving the world since 1998. They published my first articles on a holistic approach to recovery. Glenn was my editor in the early chapters of this book and he pushed me to write more, and to write fearlessly.
- Evlynne B. Householder and Robyn Shumacher, yogi master. The joy, flow of movement and integration I experience in their classes inspired my writings about yoga.
- Luis Villatoro, Printland Santa Monica, for years of support on my journey.
- my husband, Sherwyn Drucker, for his support, critique, suggestions and editing. His love made this book possible.
- Monty and Brutie, for sustaining me with their love.
- my book production team of Carolyn Porter and Alan Gadney. Carolyn's creativity and expertise in editing and Alan's knowledge and marketing expertise have been invaluable. They are wonderful people to work with.
- John Gibson of John Gibson Photography for the author photographs.

If I am able to help one single person who longs for a healthy marriage, one couple struggling in their marriage, one parent raising a child, one person tormented by their wounded Inner Child, one person searching for their Authentic *Self,* then my book will be a success.

Table of Contents

SECTION FOUR
Working Together to Achieve
a Healthy Relationship   167

SECTION FIVE
A Collection of Inner Child Work   195

SECTION SIX
Working Together to Achieve
a Healthy Marriage   239

SECTION SEVEN
Developing Relationship Skills   277

THE OLDEST SHIP

TWO YEARS AFTER MY SECOND DIVORCE, my youngest child moved out of the house, and my two cats passed away from feline leukemia. At 46, I was feeling too old to buy a pair of roller blade skates and pessimistic about ever being happily married. I had the following dream:

"I am the oldest, dullest ship in the beautiful, exotic harbor. I am brown, my paint is peeling, and there is no life or gaiety and few people in my life. The water in my pool is dark and murky. It is not clear and inviting...This water is old and smelly, and you can't see through it, and you don't want to swim in it.

This ship doesn't have a mast or sails. It has no possibility of movement. It is like an abandoned old piece of lifeless junk. There is no life or excitement on board and it seems it will be stuck here forever.

This poor ship is docked in a very exciting, lively tropical harbor. There are many pretty ships passing in and out and many docked nearby. I can hear the life and gaiety from the other ships. I want to be like the other ships."

After I recorded this dream, I did the following creative writing dialogue between the ship and me:

Judith – *"Dear, old, drab ship...I am afraid to talk to you because I'm afraid of what you'll have to say."*

Ship – *"You don't like me very much, do you?*

Judith – *"No, I don't like you. I don't like you at all. You're old and rundown and broken and lifeless… Nobody wants to be on you. Nobody wants to maintain you — most of all me."*

Ship – *"Am I so horrible? Is there no hope? Will you discard me, too?"*

Judith – *"Yes, you are horrible. You're despicable… You'd be so much work to fix up."*

Ship – *"I see you weeping as you say that…. Tell me about it."*

Judith – *"I am so tired. I just don't have the strength to do all the work required to fix you up. Your pool needs to be drained. I hate the stale smell of your water, and who knows what ugly, horrible things I would find in the pool."*

Ship – *"Yes, the water has been there a long time and it does stink and there are probably some old, dirty objects, but it wasn't always like that — and it won't have to be like that if we add new water."*

Judith – *"Yes, but there's more work involved than just adding new water. I'd have to scrub your hull, peel off the paint, and repair the cracks. Do you know how much time and effort and energy that would take?"*

Ship – *"But, Judith, I have a very good foundation. I was very well made many years ago — by a Master Craftsman — and if you examine me carefully you will see my quality. I am redeemable. I am valuable."*

Judith – "*I know you're probably right. But I don't want to do the work. I came to you for a rest, relaxation, a vacation. I don't want to do the work… I want to be on a ship that is already beautiful, that someone else has already made pretty.*"

Ship – "*But, Judith — sweet, little Judith Anne — I am* YOU. *And to have the beauty you want in life, you must do the work on your own Self. It cannot be done by another.*"

Judith – "*But, no! I want to relax. I want to rest. I am tired of work. I have been working so hard, for so long…*"

Ship – "*I know, sweet one, and I love you for it. But take heart. It's not an impossible task. And it's not more than you can handle. You will get such tremendous value and pride and satisfaction from me. I really do have wonderful potential. The strong foundation is there, don't forget, and that's the most important essential. It will be work to strip, and paint, and lacquer and polish. It will be work to build a new strong mast. It will take time to find just the right cloth for the sails. But, cheer up, you can take your time and do only as much work as your energy and courage will allow.*"

Judith – "*Well, that's a thought. It could be a project; you could become my project, my hobby. I could work on you in my leisure, as my time and energy allow.*"

Ship – "*That's a girl! Now you're talking!*"

Judith – "*And I know I am always more pessimistic when I am tired. As I relax, I get a glimpse of how you might look when I'm finished. I guess I could get into valuing myself. I guess I am salvageable.*"

Ship – "*Yes, dear, now you're talking. That's my girl!*"

3

Judith – *"Will you help me with the process? Will you show me the way? Will you talk to me and be my friend? I am so thirsty for intimacy. I don't want to be superficial and alone."*

Ship – *"Yes, little girl. I know you are fragile and vulnerable and weak right now… I know you're having a hard time. I am strong and robust and you can lean on me. Some of me is broken, but don't be misled. I am strong. I am made of solid Oak. I will rock you on the sea at night. You can rest on me and I will cradle and rock you. I love you. I will not desert or abandon you."*

Judith – *"Yes, please hold me and be there for me. I feel fragile and frightened. Hold me."*

Ship – *"There, there. Let those tears, those lovely tears flow and I will rock you. Yes, little girl, you are safe and loved and I will never abandon you. Cry, baby, cry. Cry, my sweet, sweet baby. I know the pain. I know the hurt. I know the fear… But we will both see Life and Laughter and Colors and Love again. We'll get remodeled and then we can move forward."*

Judith – *"Thank you, my sweet wonderful Ship, my Magic Ship. I'm thankful God placed me on you. I see how much wisdom you have and I am grateful. I'm so tired now. I'm going to rest."*

Ship – *"Goodnight, little girl. Sweet dreams. Rock a bye, baby."*

4

INTRODUCTION

When I was preparing for remarriage sixteen years ago, after many years of being single, I scoured the psychological literature in hopes of finding some books that would guide me. I was disappointed to find that there were few books that dealt with marriage and fewer still that had anything positive to say about marriage.

Because I was in the romantic stage of my engagement and was so busy enjoying the fun parts of the relationship, I put the books I did find down and "threw myself" into the engagement. I really wanted to believe that marriage was a good thing and that I could be successful in it. On the night before my wedding, however, I was plagued by doubts and fears. I wasn't afraid of my husband-to-be. I was afraid of my own self. As I lay in bed, tears streaming down my face, I wrote page after page in my journal, exposing my self-doubt and poor self-esteem. I already failed in two marriages. What hope did I have that I could be successful this time?

Despite my fears, I did marry my husband and was hoping so much that our marriage would be a success. It was little help to me that, shortly after returning from our honeymoon and after the first of many intermittent arguments, my husband said to me, "Maybe we made a mistake." His fears only reinforced my self-doubt. For the next three years we had some wonderful times, lots of them. But we also had plenty of issues which we had not addressed prior to the marriage, which were piling up and causing us major tension, conflict and anxiety. We had not dealt with them prior to the marriage because each of us was afraid to "cause waves" or risk losing the relationship.

As the marriage continued, each of us handled the problems with our own characteristic styles: I would express my vulnerability and needs. My husband would become frightened at the thought of having married a "weak wife" and would tell me to be quiet or "deal with it" by myself. I would respond to his rejection and indifference by becoming silent, withdrawn and angry. He would respond to my withdrawal and coldness by getting loud, sarcastic and angry. I would respond to his anger by feeling shamed and unsafe. I would stuff my feelings further down in my body and convince myself that he could not be trusted, that I would have to fend for myself. He began feeling that I was not trust-worthy. And so the foundation of our marriage was laid. We loved each other, but we did not trust each other. We had some wonderful, loving times together, but we did not talk about nor solve the major issues that were threatening to tear us apart.

We separated, in our third year of marriage. After exploring the possibility of divorce and a move to another state, I realized deep within me that I loved my husband, and that I was willing to face whatever pain our unresolved issues would bring us, in order to fight for our marriage.

I began going to individual psychotherapy and insisted that my husband join me for couple's therapy and he did. We began exchanging a series of letters and phone calls that addressed our issues and proposed solutions and compromises. We dared to face the pain and the fear. We dared to cry and hurt and shout. And we balanced the negative with once a week outings that were loving and affirming. The outings were the thread which connected us to the love we both felt for each other. We often cried on these outings. It was difficult to spend time with each other and then have to go our separate ways. But we needed the time apart.

Coincidentally, my holistic private psychotherapy practice took a new turn and brought me an influx of couples that needed care and assistance in their journeys. These couples were in various stages of their relationship: some were only dating, some were living together, some were formally engaged, some were married and so traumatized that divorce seemed the only option. Some of the couples were heterosexuals with or without children, some were gay or lesbian, some were "blended families" with step children. My couples represented a variety of economic groups, age groups, ethnic groups and nationalities. The set of common denominators that they shared were fear, confusion about the day-to-day mechanics of a relationship and an ample amount of pain. In addition, I have a number of single clients in my practice whose hearts' desire is to find the right person to marry. Many of them have been unsuccessfully married and are scarred from their divorces and subsequent years of "trial" relationships. Others are older, have never been married and are afraid that the marriages they want are "just not in the cards." Others, still, are quite optimistic about their prospects but are, admittedly, psychologically ill prepared.

In this book I want to share my own journey and the principles that I have learned from working with couples, individuals and my own husband. These principles have been hard won through years of trial and error, two failed marriages, errors made and damage caused to my own two children, pain, loneliness, doubt and searching in my own life. Many lessons were learned when my husband and I separated and seemed doomed to yet another divorce. We worked hard during the separation, straining under the weight of unresolved issues and mistrust. We felt trapped by impasses which could not be bridged. It was at that time that I asked God to help us and, coupled with our hard work, we were empowered to save our marriage.

My husband, with his love, intellect, devotion and beautiful ability to express his emotions, has taught me invaluable lessons about myself. The power of love, the knowledge of the male point of view and the give and take that is required in a marriage.

I have also learned a great deal through practicing psycho-therapy in a variety of settings: hospital work with neurology and cancer patients and their families, psychiatric work within in-patient and out-patient settings, with the homeless in shelters and a thirty year holistic private psychotherapy practice.

Perhaps the greatest teacher has been my work with substance abusers and people with a variety of addictions. The Twelve-Step program and its perspective has been invaluable in supplementing my work with clients.

I want to encourage those of you who seek love and marriage. It was the desire of my heart since I was a little girl, and it was a long time coming to my life. I firmly believe that healthy marriages are possible, and even unhealthy ones can be transformed. It is my hope that this book will give you HOPE,

COURAGE and the TOOLS to empower the achievement of your dreams. Finally, I do believe that God, however you define "Higher Power," knows the desires of your heart and wants to assist you with achieving those desires. However, God will not intervene in your life without your active invitation, which requires a certain amount of personal humility.

SECTION ONE

Preparing Yourself To Be The Best Possible Mate

"In order to fully experience love, you must first find it within yourself."

~ J.D.

Chapter 1

THE VALUE OF HARD WORK

"Having the relationship you want will not be easy. You must first work on yourself."

~ J.D.

We live in a society today that is preoccupied with immediate results. We want things that are fast and easy. We are bombarded with offers of credit cards that allow us to make purchases we cannot afford. We see pharmaceutical ads that promise to give us instant weight loss, instant sleep, freedom from depression and anxiety, relief from heartburn, pain and head aches. The cosmetic and hair care industry promise to ease wrinkles and signs of aging. Plastic surgeons can eliminate excess fat, cellulite, sagging; they can reconstruct and enhance noses, chins, breasts, eye lids, thighs and other body parts. We can purchase homes and cars with little money down.

Women can produce babies with or without husbands. Unwanted pregnancies can be terminated. No fault divorce laws have made it easy to eliminate burdensome marriages. Birth control pills allow women to have immediate sex without fear of pregnancy and without need to meet any societal expectations of commitment. People can live together without pressure to marry. Uncomfortable emotions can be drowned out by drugs and alcohol, and compulsive behaviors like shopping, eating, gambling, sex, serial relationships and workaholism. The Internet allows people to make relationships without physical contact. Written messages can be sent and received instantly by e-mail and text messaging.

As a result of this fast and easy lifestyle, we in the healing professions see a great number of people who have low frustration tolerance, inability to postpone gratification, poor problem solving skills, little self-awareness, inability to tolerate the pain that is incumbent in the growth process of a relationship. These people may look good on the outside, in terms of beauty, possessions, accomplishments, power, prestige…yet they are often ill-equipped for a healthy relationship with themselves or with another person. This is clearly visible in the increased number of divorces and broken homes, the number of people who suffer from depression, anxiety and breakdowns, the increase in drug addiction, alcoholism, eating disorders and abusive relationships. This is also seen in the people who seem to "have it all" materially, but who describe themselves as empty and emotionally starving on the inside.

In the pioneer days, there were some interesting customs which actually helped people prepare emotionally for marriage. One of these customs involved having a young woman prepare a "hope chest" for her eventual marriage. Her family would give her a large cedar chest, and then, it was her job to fill the chest with handmade items which would be needed for her marriage. It was her mother's responsibility to teach the daughter the skills required to do the work. Her mother would teach her to sew, mend, knit and quilt. As the young woman learned to do each task, she would make items that would eventually embellish her home with her husband. Over the years, with skills learned and items made, the hope chest would be filled. The young woman was also taught to cook, preserve and can, clean house, plant a vegetable garden, iron, shop for provisions and save money. The learning of these skills and the making of the items for the hope chest took time, patience and hard work. They also required humility and willingness to learn, as well as an ongoing relationship with the mother and other feminine mentors.

The by-product of this process was that the young woman's character had a chance to develop. She acquired self confidence, competence and the ability to postpone gratification, satisfaction for a job well done, self-esteem and the ability to work with others.

Young men in pioneer society were also expected to prepare for marriage. The man had to learn a trade or skill that would produce an income. He had to meet the criterion for marriage established by the parents of the potential bride. This often involved having money in savings, ownership of land and property, good reputation in the community. He often designed and built his home by hand or with the assistance of other men. As with the young woman, each of these accomplishments required time, fortitude, patience, postponement of gratification.

And with each accomplishment came self-esteem, confidence and the ability to work with other people.

For those of you reading this book who want to get married, I would like to suggest that you, too, do some preparation work. It's true that people can marry without any preparation. It's done all the time. What we see, however, is that there are many unhappy, unhealthy, unsuccessful marriages. There are many people whose hearts and spirits are nearly crushed from bad experiences in marriages. There are many people who come from broken families who are afraid to get married. There are many people who are afraid to have children because of their own painful childhoods. There are many people who stumble from one unhappy marriage into another.

My hope, *in writing this book,* is that you will make the commitment to learn everything you can to make your marriage healthy, successful and the fulfillment of your dreams. Like the transmission of AIDs, an unhealthy marriage is preventable. Even if you are currently in an unhealthy marriage, you can still do the work on yourself. It may change the course of your marriage. When you are healthier, the marriage may become healthier. At any rate, you will be able to evaluate your marriage from a healthy perspective and decide what is best for you. I counsel all people in struggling marriages to make a commitment to work on themselves as individuals and work as a couple in therapies before discarding the marriage. It's far too easy to discard an unhappy marriage, and it might not be necessary. Indeed, it might be a waste of some beautiful potential.

After doing the work in therapy, it might be apparent that the marriage will never be healthy and that you must end it. But at least you will have made an informed decision and will have learned about yourself. If you do not work on yourself and see why the marriage failed, you will more than likely repeat the same mistakes in your next relationship.

THE UNCONSCIOUS

The work I am encouraging you to do is on your "interior life," the parts of yourself which you cannot see from the outside, but which greatly influence the direction and quality of your life as a whole. They are the parts of yourself that are not discussed in the educational system, in your family or at the workplace. They are parts of yourself which have been growing from birth, just as surely as your chronological age, your height and weight. These parts dwell in your unconscious — that level inside you which is independent of your conscious, everyday mind. You may occasionally get a glimpse into this level through your dreams. The goal in therapy and the working on yourself is to bring the unconscious into your awareness so you can more fully understand yourself and can have more power over the decisions you make. To fully prepare for marriage, you must learn about all the parts of you, the conscious and the unconscious.

The UNCONSCIOUS can be understood as the reservoir inside you which contains the memories of every experience, every emotion and every person you have encountered in your entire life. Some of our life experiences have been happy and pleasurable, and we can recall them in our everyday thinking. The unconscious, on the other hand, is more likely to contain the experiences which were painful, frightening, sad, unpleasant and too horrible to remember. So they reside in the unconscious, out of sight, but with a definite life of their own. They haunt us in dreams. They consume a great deal of our physical and psychic energy to keep them hidden. They poison our relationships with ourselves and others. They frighten us and limit the range of choices we have in life. They force us to do repetitive behaviors which are damaging to our bodies and our spirits. For example, the use of drugs, alcohol and food, and the pursuit of owning things, prestige and power to drown the bad experiences out. They keep us trapped in depressions, unhealthy relationships, self-doubt and fear of trying new things. They lead us to sabotage the achievement of our hearts' desires.

To understand the importance of the unconscious, let us look at the desire for love and marriage. Many people are quite clear they want to love and to marry. What they don't realize, however, is there are forces and feelings inside them, on the unconscious level, which are frightened to death of love, commitment and intimacy. In fact, there may be definite feelings and voices inside which tell them they are unworthy, unlovable, too ugly, too damaged, and they will never receive love. These feelings and forces are equally as strong as the desire for love and marriage. So what happens is that they cancel each other out. While the person is actively pursuing love and marriage, he or she is trying just as hard unconsciously to avoid it. He or she will choose a potential mate that is guaranteed to fail.

Some examples of this would be a woman who says she wants to get married, but she will only form relationships with married men. She can pour her love and devotion into the man while being fairly well assured that he will never be available to her as a husband. She won't have to risk a deep level of intimacy with him because he will have commitments to his wife and children. Or the man who says he wants to get married but always chooses women who reject him. Or the person who desires to get married but unconsciously hates himself and pushes away anyone who tries to love him, or erects a wall around himself that no one can penetrate. Then, there are people who are always involved in "triangular" relationships, where they are involved with more than one person at a time. Or the marriages in which one or both of the spouses avoid any real level of intimacy by not talking about real issues, being constantly involved in a whirlwind of activity or work, using drugs or alcohol, using the children as a "wedge" between them, doing only independent activities or withdrawing and isolating in silence.

All these people are frightened to get the very thing they so desperately seek: emotional intimacy and commitment. They are frightened that if they bring a lover into an intimate connection, the hidden contents of their unconscious — the flaws, powerful emotions, traumatic experiences, imperfections, self-hate, — will be discovered. Unfortunately, this really does happen when we are in love. Things which are hidden from our own sight are all too quickly observed and brought to our attention by the person we love.

This can be a devastating experience to one's ego and sense of well being and safety. All the more, if our lover uses our flaws and shortcomings to shame, humiliate or control us. On some level, it is often safer to profess the desire for love and marriage than to actually pursue it. That's what happens when someone chooses a mate who is unavailable for marriage. In other instances, it feels safer to marry a spouse who does not connect than to marry someone who wants an emotional connection. In all these cases, there is an unconscious avoidance of emotional intimacy.

On the other end of the "unhealthy love spectrum," are people who throw themselves into intensely intimate relationships with mates who devalue or abuse them. They risk intimacy, but do it in an environment that is harmful to their body, mind, emotions and spirit. The reason for this destructive pattern is often found in the unconscious. These people are the ones who, on an unconscious level, do not feel worthy of the love they so desperately seek. In fact, they may feel that they deserve to be abused. They stay in abusive relationships because they are afraid to be alone with themselves or do not feel capable of being on their own.

They feel it is better to have a poor relationship than no relationship at all. The chaos of the abusive relationship serves as a "smoke screen" to avoid dealing with themselves. The day-to-day drama of the relationship prevents them from having to examine their own issues. They can blame the abuser for all of their problems and, therefore — avoid having an intimate relationship with themselves.

Then there are people in the middle of the "unhealthy love spectrum" who want to get married and receive love and intimacy, but they never date and never leave the confines of their carefully constructed life of work and home. They do not take risks. They do not join activities or accept invitations to social events. They pine away in their homes, hoping that love will find them. They are shy and often depressed or anxious. They often do not take care of their bodies. They feel negative about the world and often feel like "helpless victims." The reasons for their passive approach to love often dwells in their unconscious. They may have learned in childhood to be passive. They may have been thwarted in their attempts to receive love. They may feel that they are unlovable.

I don't know if you were able to recognize yourself anywhere on the "unhealthy love spectrum." Maybe those examples do not apply to you. Maybe you are one of the few people who are consciously and unconsciously ready to embrace love and a healthy marriage. Count yourself very fortunate. Your mission will be much easier. Some of the sections in the book may not seem to apply to you. I encourage you to read the entire book with an open mind. Perhaps something will jump out at you. Perhaps you will learn something new about yourself that will help you on your journey.

My intention is to help you build and fill your "hope chest" for marriage. Figuratively, YOU are the HOPE CHEST and I want you to learn to fill yourself with:

- knowledge of your unconscious
- understanding the impact of your childhood on your emotional/psychosocial development
- healing of inner wounds
- knowledge about how you operate in relationships
- healthy coping skills
- understanding how to be an emotionally healthy mate
- understanding how to pick an emotionally healthy mate
- techniques for working together as a healthy couple

Next, I will walk you through a journey into your unconscious. It is true that KNOWLEDGE IS POWER. Once you meet the parts of your inner life, you will understand where you are and see how you may be sabotaging your dreams You will learn to love yourself and heal yourself. Then you will be enabled to pick a mate who will love you and treat you with respect and devotion. You will be empowered to have love and a healthy marriage.

Chapter 2

FAMILY OF ORIGIN
Understanding the Damage and Unmet Needs

"No other group of people in your life has a greater impact on your emotional/psychological development than the people who raised you from childhood."
~J.D.

Of all the babies in the animal kingdom, the human baby is by far the most fragile and most dependent for the greatest length of time on his or her parents. At birth, the human baby is not able to stand on its own feet and follow the source of food like most other animal newborns. Indeed, the human baby cannot even sit up unsupported until six months, cannot crawl until seven months and generally does not walk until one year or later. Whether the baby lives or dies is entirely dependent on the parents or caretakers.

This is startlingly reflected in the current news accounts of unwanted babies dying after being discarded in trash dumpsters and public toilets. Until the human baby develops speech around age twelve months, his primary means of signaling his needs is by crying. A cry can be a call for food, comfort, a dry diaper, a stomach upset, an ear infection. If his cry goes unheeded, the baby has little recourse: He can cry again and hope that someone will come. He can eventually cry himself to sleep. Or he can learn that crying brings no help, so he may as well stop crying and stop needing.

Even as the human baby grows, he is still physically dependent on his parents or caretakers. His body is smaller than adults, he has difficulty coordinating his eye, hand, feet movements, he has no sense of danger, and he has no means of supplying his own food, shelter, clothing and medical care. His speech and vocabulary do not form in an intelligible manner unless he is taught. He lacks the mental maturity to make wise decisions on his own behalf. Yes, throughout the physical developmental stages of toddler-hood, elementary school, secondary school and high school, the human child is obviously dependent on his or her parents or caretakers. Society in general recognizes these needs and has made laws to protect children.

EMOTIONAL/PSYCHOLOGICAL NEEDS

Besides the obvious physical needs, however, there are a whole host of emotional/psychological needs which children have. Unfortunately, these needs are not widely known or understood. I believe that all children have five basic needs:

1. **Love**

2. **Safety**

24

3. **Approval**

4. **Guidance**

5. **Respectful Boundaries and Consequences**

These needs reside in the baby's body, mind, emotions and spirit. The very same needs must be satisfied for the growing child and the adolescent. The extent to which these needs are met will determine, to a great degree, whether or not the child develops a healthy self-esteem and the ability to love himself and other people. I cannot stress enough how important it is to understand these needs. To assist you, I will provide further explanation of each need:

1. Children need to know that they are loved — just because they were born and are a member of the family. They should not have to "earn" this love, nor should they be threatened with the loss of this love.

2. Children need to know that the family approves of their own unique identity.

3. Children need to know that their bodies, minds, emotions and spirits are safe within their family.

4. Children need to be guided by their family to learn skills, cooperation, development of their gifts and understanding how to function within the larger society.

5. Children need to learn respectful boundaries and experience respectful consequences when they violate boundaries.

Respectful boundaries are those which channel the child's growth and the development of his or her conscience. They teach the child about rules, rights and acceptable behavior.

Consequences for boundary violations should be "just" and should not be greater than the violation warrants. Respectful consequences do not control or restrict the child's individual identity, which may differ from the identity of the parents. Rather, they hold the child accountable for his or her behavior.

Parents need to be consistent with boundaries and consequences in order for children to learn to be respectful and to control their impulses, frustration and behavior. Likewise, parents need to administer consequences in a respectful, controlled manner. They do not have the right to violate their children's bodies, minds, emotions and spirits.

As you read this section, try to recall your growing-up years. To understand the emotional/psychological needs of children, let's begin by looking at the baby. In terms of development, the baby is, once again, entirely dependent on his parents or caretakers. In the beginning, the baby has no sense of himself as a separate entity. He looks at the face of the person who is holding him or feeding him and thinks that it is "him." In his small mind, there is no separation between that person and himself. They are both one person.

This primary caretaker, then, becomes tremendously important to the baby and his emerging self-identity. Whatever is seen in the face of the parent is mirrored back to the baby. Whatever is felt in the body of the parent is felt in the body of the baby. If the parent is happy, the baby is happy and feels good about himself. If the parent is warm and loving, the baby feels love and feels lovable. If the parent sings and talks to the baby, the baby will attempt to communicate back to the parent, feeling a sense of trust. If the parent is prompt in responding to his cries, the baby feels important. If the baby gets to feel the warmth and closeness of his parent's body, he feels safe and enjoys being touched. If the baby hears his parents' laughter, he feels the world is a good place to be. This is how the baby's initial self-concept is formed — in response to the actions, affections, attitudes of the parents. In these cases, the baby would have a good self-concept and good self-esteem.

Contrast that with what happens if the baby has a series of negative experiences with his parents? What if the mother never wanted the baby and was unhappy throughout the entire pregnancy? What if the mother neglected to get medical care during her pregnancy and engaged in behaviors that were harmful to the growing fetus? What if there was no father to support the mother during the pregnancy or after the birth or there was no other social support system for her, causing her to be depressed, anxious or distraught? What if the baby's cries were met with anger or no response at all? What if the faces the baby looked into were detached or rejecting? What if the baby was never held during feedings, but was fed by a bottle propped up on a pillow or rarely fed at all? What if the baby was left to remain in badly soiled diapers for hours or days on end? What if the parents were always high on drugs or alcohol? What if the baby was raised by hired caretakers who were indifferent? What if the baby was raised in foster care? What if the baby was raised in a home where the mother and children were abused? What if the baby was placed in the care of young siblings? What if the baby was hit or thrown or shaken violently because it continued to cry? What if the baby never received love and warmth?

There are documented cases of babies who die from "failure to thrive" because no one responded to their need for love, touch and emotional warmth. As you can imagine, any of these experiences would have a negative impact on the development of the baby. The baby would have feelings and reactions to the situations, but would not have the vocabulary to communicate them. Instead, the feelings of fear, sadness, anger, confusion, rejection, etc. are really preverbal at this age and would be placed in the depths of the baby's forming unconscious. There would be a vague feeling deep within the baby that he or she was not lovable, was not good and was not worthy. These experiences would also be registered in the memory of the body. The body would hold the emotions, much like memories of odors are stored. Have you ever had the experience of a particular odor in the present bringing to the surface a memory from the past? I have.

The best way I can describe this theory of body memory is from my own experience. In the field of bioenergetics, it is said that the lower half of the body is our "self-support" system. The upper part of our body is the part which "gives to others." Personally, my lower body is very strong and muscular — a product of being an athlete and dancer. I also believe my lower body is so developed and strong because I grew up having to support myself emotionally. As a result, when I go through traumatic experiences, the emotions of the trauma are stored in my legs and produce extremely painful cramps and, sometimes, hives. I am unable to stop the cramping, which occurs after the events have passed, until I literally give sounds to the pain and cry. My body wants me to release the painful emotions. If I do not release the emotions shortly after the traumatic event occurs, the emotions can be stored in my body memory for years.

When my Mother died four years ago, my body was filled with unbearable pain and tension at the time of her death. Despite crying and grieving, my body continued to hold the pain and tension for months. My body remembered the anguish I felt on the day she died. Because of this, I was compelled to go in for deep tissue work with my massage therapist for months, because the pain was unbearable and debilitating. I told my massage therapist about my Mother's death and told him not to be surprised if I cried a lot during my massage sessions. Sure enough, when he worked on my body, my lower back, legs and feet began to have extremely painful cramping. The cramping could not be released until I cried and sobbed.

From a clinical perspective, the body memory phenomenon can also be observed in Post Traumatic Stress Disorder. When a person experiences or witnesses a potentially fatal event or an assault to their physical or psychological integrity, the person will have intense feelings of fear and helplessness. Many times, the person will "numb" these reactions and the emotions will be deposited and stored in the body and brain.

When the person is confronted with environmental reminders of the traumatic event, the body will experience intense physiological and psychological reactions to the stimuli. The person might have trembling and shaking, chest pain, a desire to curl up in a fetal position, nightmares, etc.

An example would be a Vietnam war veteran whose body and mind have "flash backs" when he hears the sound of a helicopter. Or a victim of rape whose body memory of the event is activated when she is touched years later. Current research on the brain, using brain scans, indicate that in cases of trauma, the sights, sounds and sensations of the event are stored in the right hemisphere of the brain. If the person is unable to talk about the experience or release the effects of the event, the right brain will continue to hold this information indefinitely. The body, mind and emotions will continue to suffer.

Going back to the baby raised in an unhealthy family, on some level the baby's body would feel pain and tension. The baby might begin to withdraw from touch or dread being touched. The baby might develop a hypersensitivity and hyper vigilance to the world, tensing his body in anticipation of danger. He might have trouble falling asleep, staying asleep or be plagued with upsetting nightmares. He might become a "demanding baby," unaware that he is crying out for love. He might become shy and introverted. He might not crawl or walk or talk or explore the world around him. He might develop an eating disorder, where he will not eat or is constantly hungry. All of these behaviors would be occurring on a preverbal, unconscious level. The baby would not realize that he is unhappy or feels unloved. This "uncomfortable state" would simply feel natural and normal to him.

As the baby grows into an older child, his self-concept continues to be greatly influenced by his parents. To the child, the parents represent "God," "the world," "everything." All children instinctively love their parents and want to be loved by them. I think it is the single greatest need of every child: to be loved and accepted by his parents. Because the desire for love is so great, there is almost desperation to have the parents all to himself. Children thirst for individual time and attention with their parents. In families where there are too many children or where the parents do not offer an abundance of love, they will engage in fierce rivalries with siblings to be the most important, most loved child in the family. Much like little puppies fighting for scraps of food under the table. Parents are the CENTER of a child's universe. Children listen, watch, follow, cling, imitate. They ask a multitude of questions and want to be intimately connected to their parents in every way. Year after year, day in and day out, they soak up and absorb every aspect of their parents' world — personality, mannerisms, speech, habits, attitudes and interaction with other people. The parents and the parents' world become part of the child's emerging identity. Some of this occurs on a conscious level, and some of it occurs on the unconscious level.

Because children so value their parents and seek their love and approval, the impact that parents have on the child's self-concept and self-esteem is enormous. No other two people in life will have a greater effect on the outcome of the child's life. When he becomes an adolescent and lives through the "love/hate relationship" with his parents, where he must reject their ways in order to establish his own, independent identity, he continues to depend on his parents. He is frightened by the changes in his body and his emotions, by the expansion of his world beyond the family and neighborhood, by the possibilities and expanded choices he will have to make regarding education, employment, friendships, sex, drugs and alcohol, and by the need to grow up and leave his parents' home. He turns to his parents for love, reassurance, guidance, support, structure and approval of his budding identity.

If the parents are emotionally healthy people, capable of giving love and approval to each other and to their children, they will be positive role models for the child. They will provide a wonderful environment for growth and development. The child will learn from these parents that life is good and worth living. That love, respect and protection is a right for all family members. A father can be strong, wise, loving, as well as, vulnerable — in need of the love and support from his wife and children. A mother is a beautiful combination of strength, softness, intelligence and capability, who delights in the love from her husband and children. That a father and mother can work together to make a loving home: warm and safe for all its members. That it is normal to have needs, wants and emotions and that the family members will honor them. That it is good to express your thoughts and emotions. That it is good to be your own, distinct person. You have the right to learn and grow according to your own abilities. Family members are accountable to each other for wrong doing. That forgiveness is freely given. That conflict can be resolved in a safe manner. That it is okay to make mistakes and not have all the answers. That the family can experience and express every emotion in ways that are safe. That being loved is not something you have to earn; it is your right as a family member.

If a child is raised in this kind of family environment, he or she will develop healthy self-esteem, respect for self and others and the capacity to give and receive love. His conscious and unconscious will be filled with positive messages and positive images. He will have the confidence to grow and learn and try new things. He will not fear making mistakes. He will love his parents and will feel loved by them. Even in his adolescent years, being half-child, half-adult, struggling to establish his own separate identity, he will maintain a healthy relationship with his parents. His identity and sense of himself will be built on a healthy foundation of love and approval from his parents. This foundation being built over the years of childhood and adolescence, will allow the child to experience a life of healthy relationships and successful endeavors. Even when life brings hard, challenging times, the child will have confidence, resilience and healthy means of coping with the stress. He will be like a house whose foundation is built on rock: though the storms come, the house will not crumble, it will not be blown away.

If you were born and raised in a loving, healthy family, the probability of you having a loving, healthy marriage is great. You see, we are so influenced by our family of origin that we tend to recreate that family atmosphere in our adult relationships. We do this on a conscious and an unconscious level. As adults, we will pick people who feel familiar to us — who mirror the personalities, characteristics, culture of our parents. On some level, it's as if we are still children, searching for the familiar faces we first looked into. When we find people similar to our parents, we feel safe, "at home." You will draw to yourself people who are able to take care of your five basic needs. And you will have no fear of love and intimacy, because you have already experienced love and intimacy in your life.

By the same token, if you were raised in an unhealthy family, by parents who did not provide for your five basic needs, there is a high probability you will stumble into an unhealthy marriage. That is why I encourage you to take a good, slow look at your family of origin and its impact on you. You might initially think that everything was fine. We all want to believe that our family was good and took good care of us.

On closer inspection, however, you might discover and acknowledge that your five basic needs were not met. Or only some of your basic needs were met. Because those needs were not met, you will tend to draw people to you in adulthood who are similar to your parents. They will be "familiar" to you, and it will be like you are giving yourself a second chance to "get it right," to have those original unmet needs met by these new people. But you will be no more successful with these people than you were with your parents.

You will be a person who looks like an adult and has a certain amount of power in the external environment, but internally, on an unconscious level, you have a wounded child filled with all kinds of unknown, chaotic issues and emotions. The Inner Child will, once again, reach out to receive love, but will lack the skills and confidence to achieve it. In fact, the Inner Child might be so angry and defensive that he drives the love away. The child tries to find love in all the wrong places, with all the wrong people. The probability of you getting your emotional needs met will be slim. You are more likely to draw people to you that will incur more damage to your heart, mind, body and spirit.

Chapter 3

CHILDHOOD COPING MECHANISMS
Where They Come From and Why We Needed Them

To assist you in evaluating your family of origin, I am giving you a questionnaire devised as a vehicle for self awareness. The questionnaire asks you to provide information about your developmental process. You will revisit your early life and pull emotional, subjective information from your unconscious, as well as your conscious memory. I encourage you to take your time with each question. Try to visualize the people, the places, the situations, the events, your "*Self*" at various ages. As you read each question, breathe slowly and let your body, mind, emotions and spirit help you come up with the answers. If a question feels too scary or too difficult, move on to the next question.

Try to answer with as much detail as possible. The more you put into it, the more you will get out of it, so copy these questions and slowly write your answers. Or, you could start a Journal and put the questions and your answers in it or, you could purchase the accompanying Workbook and put your answers there.

ANALYSIS OF YOUR CHILDHOOD AND ADOLESCENCE

1. What was the culture, the lifestyle of your family? Jobs of your parents, income, location, ethnic group, religion and family activities?

2. Describe your parents' relationship. Did they seem to love each other, did they share affection, how did they handle anger and other emotions, did they get divorced, etc.?

3.   Were you a wanted child? Describe . . . .

4.   Did you receive enough love, affection and special time
      with your parents?
              As a child . . . .

              As a teenager . . . .

5.   Were you made to feel special by your parents? Describe . . .

6.   What was your role in the family? Describe the role you
      played: examples: trouble maker, sickly one, clown, people
      pleaser, social worker, high achiever.
              As a child . . . .

              As a teenager . . . .

7. Describe your personality:
    As a child . . . .

    As a teenager . . . .

8. Describe your communication style: Were you open and direct, or silent, sarcastic, indirect, superficial, hostile?
    As a child . . . .

    As a teenager . . . .

9. What "messages" did your parents tell you about yourself?
    As a child . . . .

    As a teenager . . . .

10. Describe your relationship with your mother:
    As a child . . . .

    As a teenager . . . .

11. Describe your relationship with your father:
    As a child . . . .

    As a teenager . . . .

12. Did you show love and affection?
    As a child . . . .

    As a teenager . . . .

13. What were your needs and wants?
    As a child . . . .

    As a teenager . . . .

14. Were there ways in which you were different from your family? Explain . . . .

15. Did your family honor and respect those differences? Describe how . . . .

16. How did you feel about your body? Were you too fat, thin, ugly or uncoordinated? Were you pretty, athletic? Did you have a disability?
    As a child . . . .

    As a teenager . . . .

17. How did you feel about your sexuality? Curious, pleased, proud or ashamed, dirty, couldn't touch yourself?
     As a child . . . .

     As a teenager . . . .

18. As a teenager, were you sexually active? At what age? Did you use birth control?

19. Did you experience any traumatic events? Emotional or physical? Loss of a loved one or pet? Parents' divorce? Describe the event/s and how you dealt with it/them.
     As a child . . . .

     As a teenager . . . .

20. Did you use food, drugs and alcohol, or some compulsive behavior to make you feel better?
    As a child . . . .

    As a teenager . . . .

21. How did you protect yourself from stress and danger?
    As a child . . . .

    As a teenager . . . .

22. What was your relationship with your siblings? If you were an only child, how did you feel about it?
    As a child . . . .

    As a teenager . . . .

23. What were the rules or expectations in your family? (The spoken and unspoken rules)
     As a child . . . .

     As a teenager . . . .

24. Describe your experience in the school system — grade school, middle school and high school: (grades, teachers, activities)
     As a child . . . .

     As a teenager . . . .

25. Summarize the characteristics of your friends: Did you have many friends? Was your family geographically isolated from neighbors?
     As a child . . . .

     As a teenager . . . .

26. How did you handle hurt and anger? Toward your *Self*, family or friends?
    As a child . . . .

    As a teenager . . . .

27. Did you feel safe?
    As a child . . . .

    As a teenager . . . .

28. Were you given guidance and teaching? Were your parents' patient, shaming or indifferent?
    As a child . . . .

    As a teenager . . . .

29.   What were your responsibilities, chores in your family?
         As a child . . . .

         As a teenager . . . .

30.   Were you given respectful boundaries and consequences?
         Were the boundaries and consequences too severe or un-
         reasonable? Did your parents "enable" your bad behavior by
         giving you no boundaries or consequences? Give examples
         As a child . . . .

         As a teenager . . . .

31.   What was your "philosophy of life?"
         As a child . . . .

         As a teenager . . . .

32.   What were your special interests? Hobbies, sports, movies, reading, computer, video games?
        As a child . . . .

        As a teenager . . . .

33.   Did you have any special place to go? (To hide out or just get away from it all)
        As a child . . . .

        As a teenager . . . .

34.   Did you and your parents believe in God? Did you go to church or temple or practice privately? Were you agnostic?
        As a child . . . .

        As a teenager . . . .

35.   Did either of your parents have an addictive or abusive personality? Abusing alcohol, drugs, food or some other

addictive behavior? Abusing family members or you? Explain . . . .

Did they ever get into treatment?

36. Did either of your parents or anyone in the "family tree" have a mental illness: Depression, anxiety, bi-polar disorder, etc.? If so, were they on medication or in therapy?

37. What were your strengths and special abilities? (It's OK to brag about yourself)
    As a child . . . .

    As a teenager . . . .

38. If your parents divorced and remarried, describe your relationship with your step parent(s) and any step siblings or half siblings.

ANALYSIS OF YOUR CHILDHOOD AND ADOLESCENCE:

On a scale of 1(least) to 10(most), evaluate whether your FIVE EMOTIONAL/PSYCHOLOGICAL NEEDS were met:

LOVE

1 · · · · · · · · · · · · · · · 5 · · · · · · · · · · · · · · · 10

SAFETY

1 · · · · · · · · · · · · · · · 5 · · · · · · · · · · · · · · · 10

APPROVAL

1 · · · · · · · · · · · · · · · 5 · · · · · · · · · · · · · · · 10

GUIDANCE

1 · · · · · · · · · · · · · · · 5 · · · · · · · · · · · · · · · 10

RESPECTFUL BOUNDARIES AND CONSEQUENCES

1 · · · · · · · · · · · · · · · 5 · · · · · · · · · · · · · · · 10

You have just completed a look at your family of origin and have assessed whether your five basic needs were met. Some of you will conclude that your family was healthy and all your basic needs were met. Count yourself blessed if you came from such a family. You are in the minority. Thanks to your family, you will have good self-esteem and the capacity to maintain healthy, intimate relationships with yourself and others.

A sad reality for large numbers of people is that they will realize their family was unhealthy and that most, if not all, of their needs were not met. Experiences with your family will color every aspect of your life. Then there are others who decide that their family was a "mixture" and that some, but not all, of their needs were met. This probably accounts for the highest number of families. For them, the wounding will be less severe.

THE IMPACT OF AN UNHEALTHY FAMILY

Now, I would like to show you the tremendously negative and insidious impact that an unhealthy family has on the developmental process of a child and an adolescent. I call it insidious because, on the surface, to the outside world, people may not know that anything is wrong. The baby grows into childhood. The child grows into adolescence. Physical and chronological growth is taking place. The child or adolescent looks alright on the outside. But what is happening inside the child? What is happening to the psyche, the emotions and the spirit of the child who is raised in an unhealthy, dysfunctional family? To answer these questions, I will give you some additional information that is gleaned from the field of psychology. By better understanding the process of psychological development, you will better understand yourself and the impact your family has on your life.

PSYCHOSOCIAL DEVELOPMENTAL SKILLS

In terms of "interior development" (psychological, emotional and spiritual), there are certain "psychosocial developmental skills" which all children, in every culture around the world, are challenged to master in order to have achieve healthy functioning within themselves and with other people. The mastery of these skills must be done within the context of the social environment, as we pass from one stage of life into another — from birth to old age. Erik H. Erikson, a prominent Danish psychoanalyst who trained in Vienna, immigrated to the United States, became a certified Montessori teacher and taught at Harvard Medical School and Yale School of Medicine, originated this important theory of development in his book, *Childhood and Society*. W. W. Norton & Company, Inc. and The Random House Group Ltd. have graciously given me permission to re-print selected passages from Chapter 7, "Eight Ages of Man," which I list below and in the Appendix.

"In this book the emphasis is on the childhood stages.... of the life cycle....Psychosocial development proceeds by critical steps — "critical" being a series of turning points...Each critical item of psychosocial strength...is systematically related to all others, and...they all depend on the proper development in the proper sequence."

1. Basic Trust vs. Basic Mistrust

"...Mothers create a sense of trust in their children by that kind of administration which in its quality combines sensitive care of the baby's individual needs and a firm sense of personal trust-worthiness within the trusted framework of their culture's life style. This forms the basis in the child for a sense of identity which will later combine a sense of being "all right," of being oneself...

The general state of trust, furthermore, implies not only that one has learned to rely on the sameness and continuity of the outer providers, but also that one may trust oneself."

2. Autonomy vs. Shame and Doubt

"...Outer control at this stage, must be firmly reassuring.... As his environment encourages him to "stand on his own

feet," it must protect him against meaningless or arbitrary experiences of shame and doubt…

From a sense of self-control without loss of self-esteem comes a lasting sense of good will and pride."

3. Initiative vs. Guilt

"…Initiative adds to autonomy the quality of undertaking, planning and "attacking" a task for the sake of being active and on the move…

He is eager and able to make things cooperatively, to combine with other children for the purpose of constructing and planning, and he is willing to profit from teachers…

The danger of this stage is a sense of guilt over the goals contemplated and the acts initiated in one's exuberant enjoyment of new locomotor and mental power."

4. Industry vs. Inferiority

"…He…becomes ready to apply himself to given skills and tasks… He develops a sense of industry… In all cultures, at this stage, children receive some systematic instruction…

The child's danger, at this stage, lies in a sense of inadequacy and inferiority. If he despairs of his….skills or his status among his….partners, he may be discouraged from identification with them….

This is socially a most decisive stage: since industry involves doing things beside and with others."

5. Identity vs. Role Confusion

"…in puberty and adolescence all sameness and continuities relied on earlier are more or less questioned again, because of a rapidity of body growth which equals that of early

childhood and because of the new addition of genital maturity.

The growing and developing youths, faced with the physiological revolution within them, and with tangible adult tasks ahead of them are now primarily concerned with what they appear to be in the eyes of others as compared with what they feel they are...

The danger at this stage is role confusion....

Young people can also be remarkably clannish, and cruel in their exclusion of all those who are "different," in skin color or cultural background, in tastes and gifts, and often in such petty aspects of dress and gesture as have been temporarily selected as the signs of an in-grouper or out-grouper. It is important to understand (which does not mean condone or participate in) such intolerance as a defense against a sense of identity confusion."

6. Intimacy vs. Isolation

"...the young adult, emerging from the search for and the insistence on identity, is eager and willing to fuse his identity with that of others. He is ready for intimacy, that is, the capacity to commit himself to concrete affiliations and partnerships and to develop the ethical strength to abide by such commitments, even though they may call for significant sacrifices and compromises...

The avoidance of such experiences because of a fear of ego loss may lead to a deep sense of isolation and consequent self-absorption."

To facilitate your understanding of this important theory, I will present my interpretation of the Psychosocial Developmental Skills.

Childhood Coping Mechanisms

Age 0 – 1 year	Establish Basic Trust of Others and *Self*. Trust is learned through consistent care of the baby's needs by the parents.
Age 2 – 3 years	Become Autonomous (independent from parents). The toddler works to master control of his body and the environment.
Age 4 – 5 years	Begin to Initiate, not imitate, activities. The pre-school-child directs play and social interaction and develops a conscience.
Age 6 – 12 years	Become Industrious (cope with school, learning, life outside the family). The school-age-child acquires refined skills and abilities which give a sense of pride and self-worth.
Age 13 – 18 years	Establish an Identity. The adolescent integrates many roles (child, sibling, student, sexual being) into a sense of *Self* — influenced by role models and peer pressure.
Age 19+ years	Develop emotional Intimacy. The young adult learns to make a personal commitment and attachment to another person or partnership.

These "psychosocial skills" are very important to understand when you are looking at your own development. Starting with the mastery of the first skill, all the others build on the acquisition of the first — like building blocks. The problem for all children is that they are called to master these skills within the family and the environment in which they are raised, and most families have some level of dysfunction and are poorly equipped to assist the children. If the child does not master each skill, he/she will be stunted, "fixated," stuck at the age of the skill that was not acquired and will develop its opposite characteristic. For instance,

Age 0 – 1 year	lack of basic trust = basic mistrust
Age 2 – 3 years	lack of autonomy = shame and doubt
Age 4 – 5 years	lack of initiative = guilt
Age 6 – 12 years	lack of industry = inferiority
Age 13 – 18 years	lack of identity = role confusion
Age 19 + years	lack of intimacy = isolation

If the child does not master a particular skill at a particular age, he or she will continue to grow physically and chrono-logically and may master other skills on the developmental ladder, but the skill not mastered will haunt them and keep them "child-like" — stuck at that age. It will be as if that part of them is "frozen in time." For instance, the baby, who does not master the skill of establishing trust with his parents in his first year of life, will feel scared and emotionally needy. He will have a hard time moving away from his parents at age two. He might become "clingy," not wanting to leave a mother's or father's side. He might be scared of the dark. He might not want to explore his back yard and the neighborhood kids — because he does not trust that the world is a safe place. He might be afraid to play on the playground equipment, afraid to ride his bike, afraid to attend pre-school. By not learning how to trust, he will have difficulty mastering the other tasks…or he might latch hard on to the other tasks and master them, hoping that these will make up for his lack of trust.

Or the example of a child, who has not learned to trust and is very emotionally needy, who might go in the other direction and learn to "turn off" his needs and become "anti-dependent." This child might push other people away, or might not like being touched. He might become overly stubborn and independent. He will quickly move on to master autonomy, industry and identity, but he will flounder again when it comes to intimacy — because he never learned to trust and is, therefore, afraid of intimacy. Yet, inside, he might be extremely sad and despondent because he can trust no one and can never receive the love and approval he so desperately needs.

If you think about it, you can understand how these un-mastered skills may be haunting you as an adult. Here you are, a grown-up man or woman with a certain amount of power in your environment, but, inside, there may be a one year-old-child who doesn't trust, or a two to four year old who is anti-dependent, or a five to 11 year old who thinks that if you just stay busy enough or amass enough power or money, you won't have to deal with your sadness, emptiness or lack of relationship.

UNDERSTANDING THE CONNECTION BETWEEN NEEDS AND SKILLS

I would now like to walk you through an understanding of the connection between the psychosocial developmental skills and the five emotional/psychological needs of children. It is very important to see how inter-dependent they are:

Emotional/Psychological Needs of Children	Psychosocial Developmental Skills
1. Love	1. Basic Trust
2. Safety	2. Autonomy
3. Approval	3. Initiative
4. Guidance	4. Industry
5. Respectful Boundaries And Consequences	5. Identity
	6. Intimacy

If the baby receives adequate love and safety in the first two years of life, he will probably establish basic trust with his parents and himself. He will feel that the world is a safe place.

If the toddler receives approval of his budding independence, achieves some success with bowel and bladder training and exploration of the world in the "terrible twos" — when the toddler always says "no" and wants to do it his/her own way — he or he will probably master autonomy and have good self-esteem.

If the preschooler is allowed and encouraged by his parents to initiate his own activities, is made to feel comfortable with his sexuality and is gently guided with boundaries and consequences, he will develop a conscience and a healthy relationship with his body.

If the school-age-child/adolescent/young adult receives approval of his unique identity, boundaries and consequences, and guidance from his parents, he will probably master industry, identity and intimacy, and be ready for a healthy life with meaningful, intimate relationships.

On the other hand, what happens to the Five Emotional/ Psychological Needs and the Psychosocial Developmental Skills in an unhealthy family? What if the parents do not love themselves or each other? The parents project self-rejection, anger or tension onto the child? The parents abuse drugs and alcohol? The parents are abusive: physically, verbally, sexually or emotionally? The parents neglect to take care of the child's basic needs for food, shelter, medical and dental care? What if the child's emotions, wants and needs are ignored? What if the parents give the child the message that he or she is unwanted, unlovable, defective, ugly, bad or stupid? The adolescent is never taught responsibility and is never held accountable for his behavior? Problems and emotions are never discussed? The child is not allowed to have his or her own, separate identity?

The answer to all of these questions is that the child, on some level, will be wounded and unsuccessful in mastering the psychosocial skills. The foundation on which his self-concept and identity are built will be shaky. He or she will be like a "house" that is built on sand. The storms of life will threaten to destroy his house. Every unmet need that the child has, whether it be the need for love, safety, approval, guidance, or respectful boundaries and consequences, will cause a dysfunction in some area of the child's and adolescent's development. Every un-mastered psychosocial skill will weaken his ability to function in the world.

If the child is not loved by his parents, he will not feel lovable and will not be able to love himself or trust the love from others. If the child is not safe, if his/her boundaries have been violated (body, mind, emotions or spirit), he or she will not be able to trust himself or others. This child might set up a pattern of being abused by others or abusing others. If the child does not receive approval, he will not approve of himself and will be critical of himself and others or constantly seeking approval from everyone. If he or she does not receive guidance, he or she will not gain knowledge or self-confidence. He or she might feel ashamed or might not risk trying new things, for fear of failure and humiliation. If a child does not receive respectful boundaries and consequences, he will not know how to control his impulses and will not develop responsibility or respect for others. The child will feel "entitled" to things without having to expend any effort and will expect to be "taken care of."

UNDERSTANDING THE MIND OF A CHILD

To understand how a child's mind is affected by an unhealthy family, we borrow, once again, from the field of psychology. In a lecture at Del Amo Treatment Center in Torrance, California, Colin A. Ross, M.D. stated that children between the ages of two – seven years old have the following characteristics to their thinking:

- black and white
- magical
- concrete
- egocentric

What this means is that children between the ages of two – seven do not have sophisticated minds. They do not possess abstract thinking. They think in terms of what they can see and feel with their senses of sight, taste, touch, smell, sound and feelings.

They do not understand concepts of time; they live "in the moment." They do not understand other people's motives or intentions. What they see is "what it is." They look at their world in terms of "black and white." Things are "all good" or "all bad," all or nothing, no gray areas, one extreme or the other. They see themselves as the center of the universe. Their world is "all about them." They believe that they have magical power to control people and events. They are selfish and self-centered. Their needs and wants are immediate; they do not know how to postpone gratification.

The way children's minds work is they place their parents in a "God-like" position of authority. The parents are seen as "The Source" of life itself. And for the young child, this is entirely true. The child is dependent upon his parents to take care of all his basic needs. The child believes that whatever his parents do is "Right," that they are "Good." So, if there are problems in an unhealthy family, the child believes that it has to be his/her fault. He sees himself as "Wrong" and "Bad." It would never occur to the child that the parents are damaged or incapable of giving love, safety, approval, boundaries and consequences or guidance.

Therefore, in the child's mind, if he has an unmet need, it is because he or she was not worthy of having that need met. It is his or her fault. The child blames himself because the child sees himself or herself as bad, ugly, defective, unworthy. If he or she had been good enough, pretty enough, smart enough and worthy of love, he or she would have received what was needed. The child might be angry with the parents for not giving the love or attention, but the child will continue to blame himself and believe it is his fault. The child and adolescent in an unhealthy family will continue to thirst for the parents' love, approval and guidance, only to be disappointed.

CHILDHOOD COPING MECHANISMS

The pain of wanting and needing, the pain of not getting, the pain of feeling defective and hopelessly unable to ever have his basic needs met would be almost unbearable for a child. It will be too much pain for his conscious mind and body to endure on a daily basis. The child might have fleeting glimpses that he does not like himself or that something essential is missing, but he or she will develop "mechanisms" to put most of these feelings and thoughts into the reservoir of his unconscious. He will put them "out of his mind." These mechanisms are unconscious and the child does not realize that he/she is choosing to use them to survive. In psychological terms, they are called *defense mechanisms*. These mechanisms allow us to put overwhelming thoughts and feelings out of our mind to keep us from the breaking point. Different children choose different defense mechanisms and coping styles.

Here is a list of some of them. The terms designated with a * are taken from the *Diagnostic and Statistical Manual of Mental Disorders, Text Revision, Fourth Edition,* American Psychiatric Association. The others are my own terms. I have supplied the definitions for all of them.

1. *DENIAL. Some children deny that there are problems or pain. They simply do not "see" them. They might refer to their childhood or themselves as "happy," even though they endured grave problems.

2. MINIMIZATION. Some children minimize the severity of the problem. They can talk about traumatic situations without the slightest show of emotion, or they refer to the events as "it wasn't so bad."

3.   *REPRESSION. Some children bury their thoughts and emotions in their unconscious. The thoughts and emotions become as if "frozen" in the basement of their unconscious. The problem here is that the emotions continue to generate energy and tension, which are often "acted out" in unconscious, destructive ways.

4.   FANTASY. Some children retreat from pain and problems by escaping into a fantasy world. These may be the children who "lose themselves" in reading or day dreams or play.

5.   AVOIDANCE. Some children avoid any mention or contact with the problem. They run away. They refuse to talk.

6.   *DISPLACEMENT. Some children displace their hurt or anger or rage onto people, animals and property. Bullying is an example of displaced aggression.

7.   *DISSOCIATION. Some children learn to "turn off" their bodies and their senses so that they cannot feel the pain. Some children have "out of body" experiences, where the spirit, mind, and emotions leave the body. This is typical for children who have been physically or sexually abused. Some children learn to "hide" deep within themselves, as if invisible. Some children might even develop multiple personality disorders.

8.   WITHDRAWAL. Some children withdraw from the people and events around them. They do not trust or interact with others. These are the "loners."

9.   ADDICTIONS. Some children use alcohol, drugs or sex to numb their emotions or to make their bodies and hearts "feel better." Their substance of choice is a way to fill themselves up with the love they never got.

10. DISORDERS. Some children develop eating disorders, like Anorexia or Bulimia or Compulsive Over-eating. In

these cases, food is a representation of love. They either feel starved for it and over-eat, or unworthy of it and don't allow themselves to eat.

Some children develop Major Depressions to shut down their bodies, minds, emotions and spirits. These children have low energy, are often fatigued, sleep too little or too much, eat too little or too much, have difficulty concentrating, lose interest in activities and tend to isolate themselves from others.

Some children develop Conduct Disorders, getting in trouble at school or with the law. For them, it's as if *some* attention by the authorities is better than the *no attention* they get from their parents.

Some children are chronic bed wetters, whose bladders release the tension and fear they have been holding all day. Some children stutter, bite their nails, and have nervous tics or blinking, as the result of tension and trauma.

Some children develop Anxiety Disorders. They are in a constant state of worry, live in their heads, have a "racing mind" that never stops thinking of dreadful scenarios and the need for a "back-up plan." They are irritable, on edge, don't sleep well and have muscle tension and pain. They are in a constant state of "fight or flight" reaction — where they have shallow breathing, increased heart rate and adrenaline pumping.

11. **HIGH ACHIEVEMENT/PERFECTIONISM**. Some children think they can win their parents' love and approval by good behavior. When they do not get the love and approval from their parents, they just try harder and harder to be perfect. This may not look like such a bad mechanism because these children are often high achievers, who get a lot of recognition from the environment. The problem is

that they do not get it from their parents and so they feel, inwardly, defective and "only as good as" their last achievement. Often, they report feeling like an "imposter," living in fear that they will be "found out" and rejected if people really knew them.

12. **LOSS OF MEMORY**. Some children lose memory of painful, traumatic events, sometimes not remembering years of their lives.

13. ***REACTION FORMATION**. When the basic needs are not met, children might go in the opposite direction of the need or want, disavowing that the original need or want exists. This would be the case of the needy child whose needs are not met by his parents and, therefore, becoming "anti-dependent." "I need no one for anything. I can take care of myself."

14. **OBSESSIVE COMPULSIVE THINKING OR BEHAVIOR.** Some children develop repetitive rituals or routines in an attempt to put the chaos of their world "in order." It gives them a sense of being in control of their anxiety or fear. If they count the ceiling tiles, wash their hands, lock and re-lock the doors, repeat certain routines, they will feel safe.

15. ***INTELLECTUALIZATION**. Some children learn to live in their heads, their thoughts, to avoid the feelings that live in their bodies. These children are "thinking machines" who do not have a clue what feelings they are holding in their bodies. They are shut off below the neck. They do not feel their heart, their gut reactions or the yearnings of their spirit.

16. **RAGE**. Some children use rage as a means of feeling strong and avoiding the vulnerable feelings in their bodies.

17. **BUSYNESS**. Some children deal with stress and trauma by staying in a state of perpetual motion. They are always on the move, surrounded by people, noise and activity.

18. ***ALTRUISM**. Some children escape their pain by helping others and focusing on others' needs.

19. ***HUMOR**. Some children handle their pain by finding amusement or irony in life's events and entertaining people with their humor.

20. ***IDEALIZATION**. Some children attribute exaggerated positive qualities to others, to cover up the real qualities that are hurtful.

    For instance, making a "hero" out of a father who was always working and never had any time for the child.

21. **PASSIVE AGGRESSION**. Some children find ways to in-directly express their anger. Rather than express anger directly to the person, the child might be sarcastic or damage something that belongs to that person.

22. ***PROJECTION**. Some children attribute their own uncon-scious feelings, motives and bad qualities to other people.

23. ***SELF-ASSERTION**. Some children are able to express their feelings and wants in a direct manner. This is a healthy coping mechanism.

24. **LYING**. Some children tell an untruth to cover up a wrong doing or to give an exaggerated impression of their worth in order to elevate their poor self-esteem. This might be done consciously or unconsciously.

Have a look at these defense mechanisms and see if you can identify the ones you chose as a child. They are very important for you to understand because, the defense mechanisms we chose in childhood, are unconsciously brought forward into our adult lives. What you used then to deal with pain and trauma, you are most likely using today. These mechanisms helped you survive in your childhood families and were helpful at that time. Indeed, they were the only defense you had at the time. Today, however, they are probably working against you and are counter-productive. You need to identify them, understand them, and learn new, healthier mechanisms. You are an adult now and have more choices available to you.

Even though the child uses his defense mechanisms, he or she will not be able to entirely get rid of the painful experiences from their unhealthy family. The experiences and the feelings will be "out of conscious mind" and maybe "out of conscious body," but they will continue to live inside him, in the dark world of the unconscious. The feelings and the memories will manifest themselves in inner voices which tell the child that he or she is not okay, not lovable. The voices will tell him that he is not as good as other people. The voices will remind him of his defects.

In the beginning of his development, the child might hear the negative voices and messages of his parents, which he/she takes inside him/herself and believes to be true. Later, the child will develop his own negative voice and messages. When he enters the world outside his home and experiences other people, he will accumulate even more voices and messages. Responding to this inner dialogue, the child or adolescent might insist to himself that he is, in fact, superior to other people, grander than other people. He might loudly announce to others how important and grand he is, all the while secretly doubting it himself or forced to say it often and loudly, so as to convince himself. Or he may believe all the negative inner voices and beat himself up daily, playing the negative records over and over.

REACTIONS TO NOT HAVING NEEDS MET

The tremendous unmet hunger and thirst to be loved and the pain of not being loved will reside in the unconscious. It will manifest as a hole, a void, which screams to be filled. This hole, this void can be demonstrated by the following sculpture that was made by a graduate art therapy student of mine (Joyce Emmer, Graduate Program in Marital and Family Therapy; Clinical Art Therapy, Loyola Marymount University, Los Angeles, California):

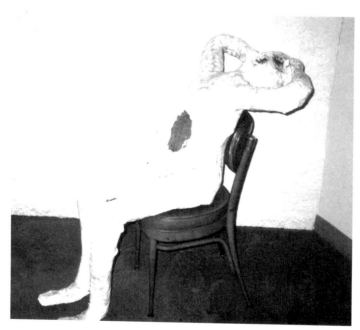

The child will be unaware of this inner void, but his outer world will reflect it. He will engage in all kinds of behaviors to fill it. He might become the problem child in the family who demands to be the center of attention. He or she might develop physical problems, ailments, illnesses which demand parental care or even hospitalizations. He might become overly dependent on the approval of his peers and be willing to do anything to obtain that approval, even behaviors which are bad or illegal. He might engage in fierce sibling battles. He might get into problems in the school system or criminal justice systems, which force his parents to give him some time and attention, figuring that even negative attention is better than no attention at all. He might turn to a gang to meet his needs for family love and approval. He might run away from home, hoping to find love and approval on the streets. He or she might turn to sex or compulsive masturbation as a substitute for family love. He might convince himself that he has no wants and needs for anyone. He might become a people pleaser, afraid to say "no" for fear of rejection.

If a child or adolescent is unable to develop adequate defense mechanisms to protect himself from unbearable pain, there will be disastrous consequences. I am thinking about cases of child and adolescent suicide. Suicide became the only recourse, the only means of escape, the only answer. Nothing else worked. The child or adolescent felt there was no hope, no possibility of change. The conscious pain, the daily assault to the body, mind, emotions and spirit were unendurable. These cases are heart breaking. They show us children caught in excruciating, silent pain and anguish. They show us children who suffered in isolation. They show us children who were damaged beyond repair. They show us children who could not trust people, the world or themselves.

Less severe examples of unbearable pain are the children and adolescents whose disappointment and pain cannot be contained in their own bodies and boils out in rage and violent behavior. Other examples are the children who mutilate themselves or those who require institutionalization for psychiatric, criminal and substance abuse disorders.

Chapter 4

UNDERSTANDING YOUR INNER CHILD

Before we leave this section, I want to give you a preliminary picture of your "Inner Child." Grasping this concept is essential to understand and benefit from the next portions of the book. In this regard, my husband asked me a really good question. "What do you mean by 'Inner Child,' and will your readers understand?"

I will try to give you a clear explanation. The Inner Child is that part of you that *was originally a child*. It is the "you" from your childhood — your first, emerging *Self*. Your Inner Child carries all your inner gifts, your original temperament, your spiritual destiny, your *Authentic Self*. Your Inner Child also contains all the experiences you had when you were growing up. It is like the acorn which goes on to become the majestic oak tree. As we age, our personality may change a bit, as our bodies do with time, or we may get lost along the journey, but I believe the Inner Child remains throughout our lifetime. I believe it is the Inner Child that contains our spirit. Try looking at old photos of yourself or reading the comments that your elementary school teachers wrote about you in your report cards. You will see that much of who you have become as an adult was visible then. (During the following exercise, I will refer to this as your *Adult*.)

Understanding your Inner Child will help you in your relationship with your *Adult* and in dealing with your potential mate, or your current spouse. I will now guide you through a "process of discovery."

Referencing the "Analysis of Your Childhood and Adolescence" Questionnaire, write down the following and circle the Emotional/Psychological needs that **were not provided** for by your parents. Put a star by the needs that *were met*.

- Love
- Safety
- Approval
- Guidance
- Respectful Boundaries and Consequences

Next, analyzing the list below, determine which of the Psychosocial Developmental Skills you **did not master.** Write down the list below and circle the ones you did not master. (Keep in mind that if you did not master a particular skill, you will feel its opposite characteristic.) Next, put a star by the skills that you *did master*. These skills will be part of your *Adult* and will reflect how you operate in the world today.

Basic Trust vs. Basic Mistrust

Autonomy vs. Shame and Doubt

Initiative vs. Guilt

Industry vs. Inferiority

Identity vs. Role Confusion

Intimacy vs. Isolation

To understand your "Inner Child" and get an appreciation of how he or she feels inside, we will now work with the following illustration and the items you circled above. Replicate this circle and text and enter the information you circled from the preceding lists:

MY INNER CHILD

**Unmet
Emotional/Psychological
needs:**

**Psychosocial Developmental
skills not mastered:**

**Childhood Coping
Mechanisms:**

If your Emotional/Psychological needs were met by your family and you mastered the Psychosocial Developmental Skills, your Inner Child will have self-esteem, confidence and the skills to connect and navigate in the outer world. If many of your Emotional/Psychological needs were not met and you did not master many of the Psychosocial Developmental skills, your Inner Child will be in turmoil. The pain and confusion of any unmet needs and skills that were not mastered will reside in the unconscious, out of your awareness. You will not feel most of the pain or know the wounds of your Inner Child because your defense mechanisms and coping styles hide them from your conscious mind.

To give you more knowledge about yourself, refer to the previous descriptions of Childhood Coping Mechanisms. Study them and try to determine which ones you used as a child. Write down the following list and circle the ones you most frequently used.

- Denial
- Minimization
- Repression
- Fantasy
- Avoidance
- Displacement
- Dissociation
- Withdrawal
- Addictions (alcohol, drugs, sex)
- Disorders (Eating Disorder, Major Depressive Disorder, Bed Wetting, Recurrent Nightmares, Conduct Disorder, Nervous Habits, Anxiety Disorder)
- High Achievement/Perfectionism
- Loss of Memory

- Reaction Formation
- Obsessive/Compulsive Thinking or Behavior
- Intellectualization
- Rage
- Busyness
- Altruism
- Humor
- Idealization
- Passive Aggression
- Projection
- Self-Assertion
- Lying

The defense mechanisms and coping skills that you circled show you the methods you used, and may still be using, to keep the pain and issues of your Inner Child hidden. As long as the pain, unmet needs and inadequacies are hidden, they cannot be healed and they will compromise the quality of your life and your relationships. Write down the defense mechanisms you *most frequently used* as a child and put them in the circle.

Finally, to take a look at your *Adult*, list the Emotional/ Psychological Needs that *were met* by your family and the Psychosocial Developmental Skills that you *did master* and starred above. These will be the strengths that you bring to your world, the people in your life and your *Self.*

MY *ADULT*

Emotional/Psychological Needs
that *were met* by my family:

Psychosocial Developmental Skills
that I *mastered:*

To understand your *Self,* I am providing this picture, which shows the *Self* as a combination of your *Adult* and your "Inner Child." Generally, the *Adult* is the part which we show to other people. Your "Inner Child" is more likely to be hidden inside or shows up when you are under stress.

MY *SELF*

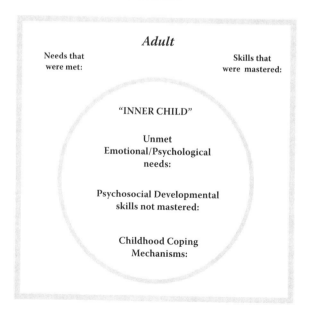

Adult

Needs that
were met:

Skills that
were mastered:

"INNER CHILD"

Unmet
Emotional/Psychological
needs:

Psychosocial Developmental
skills not mastered:

Childhood Coping
Mechanisms:

If you were raised in a healthy family, your Inner Child and *Adult* will be peaceful and compatible. Your Inner Child will not be hidden from you. You will have good self-esteem and the skills to have healthy, fulfilling relationships. You may have chosen some of the more functional, healthy defense mechanisms, because there was little internal pain and turmoil and you felt competent in the outer world.

On the other hand, if you were raised in an unhealthy family, your Inner Child will be hidden from you, because of the defense mechanisms you had to use to protect yourself from feeling the pain. This lack of connection to your Inner Child will cause you problems with your *Adult* and your functioning in the world. Fortunately, when the Inner Child is discovered and loved by the *Adult*, healing can take place and inner and outer growth will occur.

Finally, sometimes even children raised in unhealthy families have good self-esteem and successful functioning in the outer world, due to the defense mechanisms they chose or people outside their family who helped them. Their Inner Children, however, and the residual issues from their families may still cause problems in their relationships.

Chapter 5

A "HOLISTIC" COMMITMENT TO YOUR SELF
Why it is Your Responsibility and How to Do it

Hopefully, you were able to identify some of the defense mechanisms and coping skills you used when you were a child or adolescent. We have all used some of them. We needed them when we were children because we were small and didn't have much power in our environment. They helped us survive. They helped us deal with pain and discomfort.

Unfortunately, we tend to use the same childhood coping mechanisms in our adult life. After all, we've used them for a long time and they are familiar to us, much like our families of origin are familiar to us. In adulthood, however, these mechanisms usually work to our disadvantage. They are no longer our best choice. We are older now and have more options and power in our environment. What helped us in childhood often cripples us in adulthood. They prevent us from being aware of our emotions, our bodies, our thoughts and our spirits. They keep us trapped in cycles of repetitive, dysfunctional behavior. They prevent us from opening our hearts and establishing loving, healthy relationships. We cannot change these mechanisms, however, unless we are aware that we use them. And we will not stop using them until we are ready to face the hidden contents of our unconscious.

If you left your childhood and adolescence without having received your parents' love and approval or without having your other basic needs met, you will be wounded in many ways. Your relationship with your *Self* and others, your relationship with your body, your endeavors, your emotions and your perceptions of yourself will be impacted for years to come. You have carried into adulthood a wounded Inner Child who is locked in the basement of your unconscious.

Even though you may have completed the educational system, have established yourself in a career and are living on your own, there is a frightened child inside you who is unhappy and screaming for love. If you are not aware of the Inner Child and do not complete the work necessary to free yourself, the Inner Child will sabotage your relationship with your *Self* and others and will rob you of your full power, which is rightfully yours.

Your body will be fatigued and stressed from the negative memories and emotions you have stored in your unconscious. Your immune system will become depressed and you will be susceptible to illness. You may abuse your body with food, alcohol and drugs. Feelings that were repressed and "frozen" in childhood will break to the surface and cause you to react out of proportion to current situations. You will view people and circumstances with distorted thinking, assuming that people are "out to get you." You will live in your head, cut off from your heart, emotions and spirit. The unconscious defense mechanisms of the child will keep you bound up and cut off from your full personhood.

The person that you draw to yourself in love and marriage will be a reflection of your degree of emotional/psychological health. If you learn to take care of your own body, mind, emotions and spirit, if you learn to love and provide for your Inner Child, if you learn new coping skills, you will draw a similar mate. If you deny the existence and avoid your wounded Inner Child, you will draw to yourself another wounded child. You will be two wounded children, trying to "fix" each other or hoping that love will "fix" you both.

I encourage you to work on yourself, to have the courage to face your early life. No one else can do this work for you. It is your life and your responsibility. The benefits will be enormous. It is the best and most efficient use of your time and your money. It is an investment in yourself and the dividends are great. It is your "spiritual hope chest" for a healthy life and a healthy marriage. What you give to yourself can never be taken away from you.

A HOLISTIC APPROACH

I believe we are a "four-part" person: body, mind, emotions and spirit. Each part of you is important and requires attention. Each of the parts has an impact on the other parts. If you neglect one part of your *Self*, you will create a state of "dis-ease," which will manifest in some sort of symptom: illness, being over or under weight, depression, anxiety and other mood disorders, addictions, acting out behavior, spiritual bankruptcy and cynicism, isolation, fear of being alone, compulsive behavior, inability to sustain emotional intimacy. Children from unhealthy families have been wounded in their body, mind, emotions and spirit.

After thirty-three years of providing psychotherapy in a variety of traditional and non-traditional settings, studying Jin Shin Do acupressure, cancer counseling, Jungian psychology, substance abuse treatment techniques and yoga, and embarking on my journey of spiritual inner healing, it is my sincere belief that in order to heal the whole person, a holistic approach must be used — one that treats the body, mind, emotions and spirit. It must be comprehensive. When only one part of the person is treated, for instance the mind, the other parts of the person will continue to carry the problem. Most treatment approaches in our society are one or two dimensional. I will give some examples.

In most hospitals, people's bodies are treated by the medical team, often without encouraging the participation of the patient. The needs of the patients' minds, emotions and spirits often go unheeded. Licensed clinical social workers, when they are available, provide excellent treatment for the emotions and minds of the patients and their family members, but are constrained by the short length of stay allowed by insurance companies and the pressures of discharge planning.

Many patients do not know about the availability of medical social workers and never receive their help. Psychiatric consultations may be provided if the patient has a co-existing psychiatric diagnosis, but the treatment is usually limited to the prescription of psychiatric medications and referrals for mental health services. Unless the hospital has a religious affiliation and provides pastoral counseling and a chapel, the spirit goes unnoticed. Some enlightened hospitals are beginning to offer alternative forms of treatment: biofeedback, yoga, acupuncture, macrobiotic foods and spiritual counseling, but, sadly, this is generally reserved for the oncology and hospice units. If problems with the emotions, mind and spirit of the patient go untreated, there is a high probability that the medical problem will persist or reappear — often in a more critical manner.

In traditional psychiatric in-patient programs and mental health clinics, the emphasis is on treating the mind and the brain neurochemistry with medications, and using individual and group therapy to address emotions and educate the patients about their disorders. The body may be referred for treatment of medical problems, but there is generally no use of yoga, even if some other forms of exercise are provided. Generally, no one evaluates the status of the spirit or discusses spiritual healing. With this limited approach, disorders may be chronic and long-term. There are a few enlightened institutions which are beginning to offer a more holistic approach to treatment. They are documenting very successful, improved outcomes.

The bulk of transformative work on the *Self* is done in long-term psychotherapy. A variety of professionals provide psychotherapy: psychiatrists, psychologists, licensed clinical social workers and marriage/family therapists. By and large, they do a very good job. In traditional individual psychotherapy, therapists use a variety of techniques to engage the mind and emotions of the client. Most therapists focus on family of origin issues and teach their clients how to recover from wounding by using their minds and new, healthier coping mechanisms. Clients are taught how to communicate, look into themselves and solve their current life problems. They are taught about their mental health disorders and encouraged to take a proactive approach to their lives. Self-help books, journaling and "homework" assignments are used to enhance the therapy.

Emotions may be experienced through role playing, Gestalt exercises or art therapy, but the body and spirit are generally over-looked. The education for most therapists does not include the areas of the body or the spirit. As a result, therapists with an interest in those areas must seek specialty training after their graduate education. Some therapists treat the body, mind and emotions with alternative techniques like massage, E.M.D.R., relaxation techniques, guided meditation and yoga, but very few therapists explore the spirit and spirituality. Few mention the power of spiritual healing and few encourage the development of the spirit. Jungian trained therapists and analysts come closest to addressing the spirit, mainly through dream analysis and creative writing. When only the mind and emotions are treated in therapy, clients may be left with feelings of pessimism and fatalism about their disorders.

Traditional substance abuse residential and out-patient treatment programs do a good job of detoxifying and stabilizing the addicted body and brain, educating about triggers and relapse prevention and introducing the Twelve-Step approach to recovery. People are encouraged to explore their own spirit and seek a connection to Higher Power, and they are encouraged to work the Twelve Steps and get a sponsor. They are taught to take responsibility for their own recovery.

On the other hand, these programs often fail to address the underlying mental health disorders and codependency issues. After a period of sobriety, there are often relapses because the pain of mental health disorders and codependency is too great, and relief is sought from the drug of choice. These programs, also, rarely discuss how to keep the body healthy. The best results in recovery are obtained when there is a combination of recovery-based treatment and the provision of mental health treatment. Places that provide this combination are called "Dual Diagnosis" units.

In the sections which follow I am going to present you with a holistic model for healing your body, mind, emotions and spirit. All of these methods, used in conjunction, will help heal your wounds from childhood and enable you to live a healthy, abundant life. When you are healthy on every level, you will attract a healthy mate. I encourage you to take a holistic approach to your life.

1. HEALING THE BODY

There are many ways to heal a wounded body: Massage, deep muscle work and body-mind therapies, to penetrate the layers of body tension, free the emotions and memory and normalize breathing. E.M.D.R. therapy (eye movement desensitization reprocessing) is proving to be successful in moving traumatic body memory from the right brain to the left brain, where it can be released and integrated. Acupressure and acupuncture, to circulate the flow of energy, chi. Classes in yoga, T'ai Chi, martial arts, which focus on breath, energy and meditation.

I personally believe that yoga is one of the very best things you can do for your body, mind, emotions and spirit. In yoga, you learn to establish slow, deep breathing which quiets the racing heart and mind and nourishes the body with healing oxygen. As you breathe deeply and slowly, your muscles begin to relax and tension is released. The various yoga postures help your spine become flexible and maintain youthfulness in your body and spirit. In the postures, internal organs are massaged and relaxed, helping to increase the flow of energy and aid in digestion. As you gain flexibility, your muscles become elongated and compressed vertebrae are given space in the spinal column.

In yoga, you learn to be "in the moment" — worry and stress are suspended. As you lie on your mat listening to relaxing music and the voice of the yoga instructor, you enter into a state of quiet mediation and peacefulness. In "child pose," you surrender to mother earth and feel her support of your body, mind, emotions and spirit. Yoga is also strength building. Through the various postures, you build strength in your "core," arms, legs and feet. In "downward facing dog" and some other inverted postures, blood flow and oxygen are sent to the brain and face, invigorating them.

In the quiet meditative practice of yoga, you become sensitive to messages from your body, mind and emotions, which helps you learn to hear your inner voice and the needs of your spirit. Depressed emotions are released and replaced with a sense of well being. When you finish the yoga session, you feel revived and ready to return to the demands of your life. Yoga can be learned and practiced by any one, at any age.

I also recommend all forms of dance and movement. Consultation with a nutritionist, for a healthy, low-fat diet rich in fruits and vegetables, as well as herbal and vitamin supplements. Regular medical and dental check-ups. Regular exercise program which includes a cardio-vascular workout, stretch and weight work will give you the release of natural "feel good" endorphins.

Other forms of exercise that give the Inner Child a chance to play: walking, running, hiking, kite flying, cycling, swimming, tennis, volleyball, ice, roller and in-line skating, skiing, snow boarding, golf, rock climbing, surfing, hang gliding, bungee jumping, hockey, etc. They are good for the body, mind, emotions and spirit. They return us to our childhood and ease away the stress and tension in our adult lives. They envelope us in the elements of nature: air, wind, sunshine, water, snow, ice, mountains, trees, flowers, birds and other wild life, sunrises and sunsets.

Long walks with your dog give both of you a chance to bond and smile, socialize with neighbors and other dogs, and begin and end your day on a positive note. Experimentation with new hair styles, fashions and colors can enliven us. Prayer for chronic or life threatening medical problems and problems of daily life can lead to healing and stress reduction. I also recommend gardening — which grounds your body to the healing elements of mother earth, rewards your spirit with the beautiful plants and vegetables which you raise and blesses your community.

2. HEALING THE MIND AND EMOTIONS

To work on the mind and emotions, self-help books and classes can be a wonderful way to start. They give you general knowledge and a broad scope. I will provide you with an extensive bibliography of books which have helped me through the years and which have been recommended by my clients. For the deeper work, I recommend individual psychotherapy and couple's therapy with a well trained, healthy professional. Books and classes can provide you with information and exercises, but if you have been wounded in childhood, you will need assistance with the actual "process" of inner exploration, healing and transformation. I recommend that you make a one-year commitment to therapy, which generally follows a once a week schedule. It took years for you to be raised in an unhealthy family and to acquire multi-level scars. It will take at least a year to change and grow. There is no "quick fix." People who drop out of therapy prematurely rarely have lasting or far-reaching benefits.

The therapist will guide you on your journey into health. He or she will provide the "safe place" to meet and nurture your Inner Child. The therapist will teach you new, healthy-adult coping skills and will help you discard the dysfunctional defense mechanisms and toxic experiences from your childhood. The healthy, trusting relationship that you establish with your therapist, week by week over the course of that year, will then transfer to other areas of your life. You will be better equipped to talk on an emotional level of intimacy, you will have acquired problem solving skills and you will have experience with maintaining a sustained, healthy relationship.

I recommend journaling (daily writing about the experiences of your body, mind, emotions and spirit), dream analysis and art therapy as adjuncts to psychotherapy. They are "experiential mediums" which help you access your unconscious and release your spirit. They by-pass the intellect, which often screens and sensors messages that want to come from other parts of you, such as emotions, body and spirit.

BENEFITS OF GROUP THERAPY

Group therapy is another powerful tool for personal growth. It gives those of us who were raised in dysfunctional families an opportunity to experience the dynamics of a "functional, healthy family." The Group provides a safe environment where members receive love and approval of their needs and wants and we get to practice healthy coping skills in communication, problem solving, setting boundaries and dealing with the full range of emotions. Members have the opportunity to share the "secrets" they have discovered about their past and why they have poor self-esteem. They can be released from the shame and guilt, while receiving love and support. They experience the healing benefits of laughter and trust-building, and learn tools for establishing and maintaining intimacy.

DISRUPTIONS IN BRAIN CHEMISTRY AND USE OF MEDICATIONS

For some of you, therapy may not be enough. Some of you, through "genetic pre-disposition" (inheritance from the family gene pool that makes your body pre-disposed to developing an illness or disorder) and modeling from your parents, may have inherited a tendency to develop a psychiatric mood disorder and may need psychiatric medication to assist you in establishing a healthy mind and body.

Others of you may develop a single episode of depression or anxiety, in reaction to an event in your life (a divorce, an abusive experience, a life-threatening event such as the terrorism in New York City on 9-11-2001, a "down-sizing" loss of employment or housing, etc.) As a result, there may be a disruption in your brain chemistry (neuro-transmitters do not release enough Serotonin, for instance), your cerebral cortex (the "executive functioning," computer-like area of your brain) may not be able to handle the receiving and processing of your impulses, and your body will be flooded with emotions that it cannot handle. Even though you try with all your might to get "out from under it," you will be stuck in this state for months and sometimes years and will need the assistance of a psychiatric evaluation and monitoring of medication to help you return to a level of higher functioning.

There used to be a negative stereotype attached to mental illness and psychiatric medication, but this is waning, due in large part to education, people sharing and pharmaceutical ads in the media. Clearly, one third of my clients are on a combination of medication and psychotherapy, which offer the best prognosis and success with the mood disorders.

What has also "stemmed the tide" of more people being on medication is the great new host of psychiatric drugs to choose from: they are much gentler, more effective in regulating the brain chemistry and have far fewer serious side effects than the drugs used twenty years ago. All of my clients who are on psychiatric drugs are high achieving, creative, neat people. Many of them are on drugs for only a short duration, but even those with chronic disorders are very pleased with the changes the medications bring to their lives and functioning.

I will list the most frequent mood disorders and their symptoms, to assist you in your self-assessment, taken from the Diagnostic and Statistical Manual of Mental Disorders, Text Revision, Fourth Edition, American Psychiatric Association.

DYSTHYMIC DISORDER
(Formerly known as a Mild Depression)

- *Depressed mood most of the day, for more days than not, for at least 2 years*

- *Presence, while depressed, of two or more of the following:*

  1. *poor appetite or overeating*

  2. *insomnia or sleeping too much*

  3. *low energy or fatigue*

  4. *low self-esteem*

  5. *poor concentration or difficulty making decisions*

  6. *feelings of hopelessness*

Many times this disorder does not require psychiatric medication and can be treated by psychotherapy alone.

GENERALIZED ANXIETY DISORDER

The excessive anxiety and worry are associated with three (or more) of the following six symptoms (with at least some symptoms present for more days than not for the past 6 months)

  1. *restlessness and feeling keyed up or on edge*

  2. *being easily fatigued*

  3. *difficulty concentrating or mind going blank*

  4. *irritability*

  5. *muscle tension*

6. *sleep disturbance (difficulty falling asleep or staying asleep or restless unsatisfying sleep)*

It is quite common to see a person coming to therapy with a combination of Dysthymia and Generalized Anxiety Disorder. They seem to be like "cousins." If the anxiety is severe, unrelenting and crippling, medication is generally required.

MAJOR DEPRESSIVE EPISODE

Five (or more) of the following symptoms have been present during the same 2-week period and represent a change from previous functioning:

1. *depressed mood most of the day, nearly every day*

2. *markedly diminished interest or pleasure in all, or almost all, activities most of the day, nearly every day*

3. *significant weight loss when not dieting or weight gain*

4. *insomnia or sleeping too much nearly every day*

5. *body feeling slow or hard to move around nearly every day*

6. *fatigue or loss of energy nearly every day*

7. *feelings of worthlessness or excessive or inappropriate guilt*

8. *diminished ability to think or concentrate, or indecisiveness, nearly every day*

9. *recurrent thoughts of death, recurrent thoughts of suicide without a specific plan, or a suicide attempt or a specific plan for committing suicide*

The intensity of this disorder tends to numb or "freeze" the person's body, mind, emotions and spirit for long periods of time. Even the simplest of daily tasks are impossible to complete. Psychiatric medication combined with psychotherapy is the best treatment. Without treatment, the person is at highest risk of suicide when they get a sudden burst of energy, energy enough to carry out their plan.

PANIC ATTACK

A specific period of intense fear or discomfort, in which four (or more) of the following symptoms developed abruptly and reached a peak within 10 minutes:

1. *palpitations, pounding heart, or accelerated heart rate*

2. *sweating*

3. *trembling or shaking*

4. *sensations of shortness of breath or smothering*

5. *feeling of choking*

6. *chest pain or discomfort*

7. *nausea or abdominal distress*

8. *feeling dizzy, unsteady, lightheaded or faint*

9. *de-realization (feelings of unreality) or depersonalization (being detached from oneself)*

10. *fear of losing control or going crazy*

11. *fear of dying*

12. *numbness or tingling sensations*

13. *chills or hot flushes*

A panic attack could be caused by specific or imagined fears or past experiences of trauma (as in the case of Post Traumatic Stress Disorder). Medication is generally needed to relieve the severe anguish, as well as psychotherapy and relaxation techniques.

HEALING ADDICTIONS

For those of you with addictions, Twelve-Step recovery programs can provide invaluable assistance in your healing and growth and are a good adjunct to psychotherapy. There are a variety of Twelve-Step programs to choose from: Alcoholics Anonymous, Narcotics Anonymous, Cocaine Anonymous, Over-Eaters Anonymous, Marijuana Anonymous, Gamblers Anonymous, etc. There are meetings for Adult Children of Alcoholics, Codependents, Spouses and Families of Alcoholics (Alanon), etc.

Twelve-Step programs, which are the most successful means of recovering from substance abuse, are a form of group therapy. The relationship you build with your sponsor and members of the fellowship is an invaluable way to meet your emotional/psychological needs and master psychosocial skills. Letting go of denial, confronting the addiction, working the Steps, writing the personal inventory, making amends, establishing a trusting relationship with a sponsor and the fellowship, and drawing on the love, approval, guidance and strength of the "Higher Power" are all viable ways to meet your five basic needs.

Whatever path you choose, you must learn to give yourself the love, approval and care which your family of origin was not able to give you. You must clean out the toxic contents in your unconscious, in order to have room inside you for health and love. You must free your Inner Child so that she or he can return to you the gifts of the child: love, enthusiasm, creativity, energy, trust, hope, faith, spontaneity and joy.

3. FINDING YOUR SPIRIT

When you free your Inner Child, you will also release your spirit — that part of you which is individual and unique, which has tremendous power, which is designed to guide you in the process of actualizing your divine destiny. Your spirit is the most transcendent part of you. It does not age or decay, it does not die and it always seeks your highest good. It often knows what you should do before your mind, emotions and body have figured it out. Your spirit may have been cramped, battered or abused by your family of origin, but it cannot be extinguished, even in death. It is the best and most permanent part of you. It is the strongest part of you.

Your spirit can help heal you of your wounds, however severe they may be. It seeks to connect you with your Higher Power, but will always give you the right not to. Your spirit will speak to you in dreams, in writing, in art, in dance, in nature, in animals. When you are quiet, when you make time to listen, it will speak to you in a quiet inner voice. The emerging voice of the spirit does not have the negative characteristics of the internalized voices from childhood; the voices that put you down, criticized you and told you that you were worthless or ugly or defective. Your spiritual voice will give you only messages of love, approval, encouragement, hope, inspiration, creation and forgiveness. It will caution you to avoid danger and wrong doing. It will confront you when you have done wrong and call you to make amends. Your spirit, you see, can provide all your five basic needs: love, safety, approval, guidance, respectful boundaries and consequences.

The Creator has given you all the tools for a happy life and a happy, healthy marriage. Everything you need is within you. You have only to look. I firmly believe that even the most severely wounded person can be healed and can go on to establish a loving, healthy marriage and a full, abundant life.

SECTION TWO

Sharing My Developmental Process

*"The fear and the pain of the Inner Journey
are rewarded with the joy of transformation."*

~ J.D.

INTRODUCTION TO SECTION TWO

To help you understand the theories I have given you and why the work I am calling you to do is so important, I will share some of the "nuts and bolts" of my own developmental process. I will show you my family of origin, the defense mechanisms I chose as a child, and how they affected me, my marriages and my children. I will give you a look at my Inner Children. (You may be surprised that I said "Inner Children." Some of you will discover only one Inner Child. Others of you will find that you have several.)

I have conceptualized three distinct Inner Children whose "sub-personalities" existed inside me. (These Inner Children are not to be confused with a multiple personality disorder. Rather, these Inner Children represent stages of development that were not mastered, parts of the psyche that were wounded or dominant coping mechanisms.) My hope is that this sharing will put some "flesh and bones" to the theories and encourage you to look at your early life and its impact on you as an adult.

Chapter 6

MY FAMILY OF ORIGIN

I am still learning about the impact that my family of origin had on me. It is like peeling the layers of an onion or unraveling a ball of twine with a thousand knots. What I now understand about my family is that it was neither all good nor all bad. At the same time, many of my basic needs were not met and my Inner Children were wounded on many intricate levels.

My father was raised on a prominent Wyoming sheep ranch, the son of original pioneers who had settled there in 1887. His grandfather had been a preacher. My mother came from an almost identical background, but she was raised on a cattle ranch. After earning degrees in Animal Husbandry and Genetics, and then several years working in a sheep breeding program with the Navajo in New Mexico, my father changed his direction and became a career officer in the military.

I was raised in this military family. My father was a high ranking officer and my mother was his social help-mate. Together, they gave the best parties, were the best dancers, cooked the best food, had the most friends. Our house was filled with their friends, who were neat, interesting people. I had a great exposure to the world of adults and always felt comfortable around older people. My father's career afforded us an exciting, glamorous life-style. I experienced many cultures and people and had opportunities that were wonderful and enviable. In that regard, my childhood was blessed and magical.

By the same token, on a very basic level, my five Emotional/ Psychological needs were not met or were only partially met. What was missing for me in my childhood and adolescence was emotional intimacy with my parents, approval of my separate identity and respectful boundaries and consequences.

Because of my father's career, social rules of etiquette were extremely important to both my parents. Carrying oneself well in public and earning the admiration and approval of others were key. My parents were concerned with my outer appearance and aptitudes, but were not concerned about my internal development; my personal feelings and needs. I received lessons in dance, ice skating, tennis and golf, and a good education, all of which they paid for. However, we did not talk about feelings, and I was never encouraged to bring friends to the house. There seemed to be an unspoken message not to; so I didn't. I can't remember a birthday party as an older child where I was allowed or encouraged to invite friends. It's as if I belonged to my parents for their enjoyment.

Any real development of my individual spirit occurred away from home. I visited and spent the night in the homes of other children. I played extensively in nature — exploring, building tree forts (which were "safe houses"for me), or playing games with the neighborhood kids. Usually, I had one friend, who was a boy. Often, however, I played by myself in nature. That's where I felt safe. In middle school, my most intimate relationship was with a life-size baby doll, named "Tonta."

When I finally made great friends in early high school, it was heart wrenching when we had to move. At the next high school, it took me a year to break into the tight cliques and school activities. That was one of the most traumatic experiences of my life; being an "outsider," with no friends and no school activities. I chose to channel my sadness and depression into studying hard at school, making the tennis team and working with migrant farm children. I would say that my spirit led me to make those decisions, and they changed the course of my life.

My parents were not especially interested nor instrumental in my development at school. I learned to navigate the school system on my own. Studying, campus activities were all self-initiated. Going to church, singing in church choirs, thinking about God were driven by my own spirit. We were not a religious family.

My father was very loving and involved with us kids when I was a child, but later in my life he was very self-absorbed and indifferent. He did not like my questioning mind and individual spirit. The boundaries and consequences he imposed on me as a teenager were unjust, unreasonable and drastic. They were concerned with how others would view him; not concerned with my personal development. He did not give me any boundaries about dating, which left me feeling unimportant and unprotected. He did not follow my scholastic achievements or campus leadership activities. As an adult, he rarely came to visit me in my home. If I wanted to see him, it was I who had to make the effort. On his death bed, I had to ask him, "Dad, do you love me?" I was surprised when he said, "Of course I do."

I have an older brother. I always loved him, but we were never particularly close. We were more like acquaintances. As elementary school children, we were often left alone at night when our parents went to parties. This was frightening and traumatic for me, intensified by the tension in my parents' relationship. My brother and I benefited when we spent summer vacations at our relatives' ranches in Wyoming. There, we experienced some emotional intimacy and guidance, from our grandmother, aunt and uncle and their large family of six kids. On the ranches, we worked together in fields during haying season and spent time eating, talking, singing and playing cards with the family. We rode horses, went fishing, swam in the irrigation ditches. It was idyllic and just what my spirit needed. I developed a good work ethic and self-confidence working as a ranch hand — handling the same equipment, completing the same tasks and earning the same salary as the men.

My relationship with my mother was the most complex relationship in my life. I did not realize until her death that I have spent my entire life trying to gain her love and approval. When she died, I was profoundly sad and devastated — having "earned" that love, approval and intimacy very late in my life.

It is hard to explain my mother. She was a very complicated, contradictory person. She was beautiful, vivacious, intelligent, witty, competitive and extremely competent at bridge and golf, yet she had poor self-esteem. She dressed beautifully, and I loved to look at her and her clothes. You could easily say that I idolized her. She masterfully managed all the moves and setting up our households, yet she did not teach me to clean, iron, sew and bake. It was easier and more efficient for her to do the work herself than to teach me. She could be warm, funny and loving, but also harshly sarcastic and critical.

She was extremely confusing throughout my life. She was like a beautiful rose that I admired, who continually pricked me with her sharp thorns. I never felt safe. She applauded my accomplishments, but disapproved of my emotions, my exuberance and my individual spirit. She was extremely loyal and generous financially, yet very possessive, controlling and a demanding perfectionist.

I emerged from childhood and adolescence completely at odds with myself. Consciously, I felt strong, intelligent and competent. Unconsciously, I was filled with fear, doubt, mistrust, loneliness, anger and sadness. I was a time bomb that would eventually explode. I received very mixed messages about my worth from my family. I felt a lot of confusion as to whether or not I was loved or lovable. At age 10, I left notes around the house for my parents: "Do you love me? Yes_____No_____Maybe_____."

Because we moved so often, I constantly had to say goodbye to friendships and prove myself in the new school and the new environment. I chose to cut off my vulnerable feelings and concentrate on high achievement in each new setting. Despite my defenses, I was hounded by violent nightmares, sleep walking and episodes of uncontrolled coughing. By day, I was in the role of the "pseudo adult" child, mature beyond my years and bent on taking care of the other family members.

Some of the unofficial, dysfunctional rules and views of my parents were:

"If you can't do it right the first time, don't do it at all."

"If you can't say something nice, don't say anything at all."

"Social norms and rules of etiquette are more important than the needs and feelings of the family."

"Always look and perform well in public."

"Order in the house is more important than the needs and feelings of the family."

"It's better to be a boy than a girl."

"Sex is not really a good or nice thing."

"The wants and needs of the parents are more important than the wants and needs of the children."

"Strength is good, weakness is bad."

"You are too serious. You will be difficult to live with."

As a result of these messages, I developed my own set of inner rules as a child:

"Vulnerability is a liability and should be avoided at all costs."

"Trust no one."

"The only place I am safe is in nature."

"Don't ask anyone for help."

"Never show emotion on your face."

"Don't cry."

"Never make a mistake and never admit it if you do."

"You must be perfect at everything."

"You must be a winner. It's bad to be a loser."

"You must take care of everything by yourself."

"You can depend on no one but yourself."

"You are not allowed to be weak."

"You must perform all things as well as a man."

"Men are not to be trusted."

"I am different than my family; therefore I am defective and ugly."

By the time I was 16, we had lived in six different U.S. cities and two foreign countries. At school, I was adept at making friends (though I stayed on a superficial level) and establishing myself as a scholar, cheerleader and campus leader. I maintained the same pattern in college, becoming head cheerleader and an even more honored campus scholar/leader. Unfortunately, all my development was in the "outer world."

Chapter 7

MY INNER CHILD/CHILDREN

If I complete the same assignment I gave you in the previous Section, the Circle of my Inner Child/Children would look like this:

MY INNER CHILD/CHILDREN

Unmet Emotional/Psychological needs:

Love (partially), Approval, Safety, Guidance (partially), Respectful Boundaries and Consequences

Psychosocial Developmental skills not mastered:

Basic Trust, Identity, Intimacy

Childhood Coping Mechanisms:

Repression, idealization, displacement, dissociation, nightmares, high achievement/perfectionism, loss of memory, reaction formation—becoming a "tomboy" and "anti-dependent," rage and altruism

Looking at my *"Adult,"* these are the Emotional/ Psychological Needs that *were met* by my family and the Psycho-social Developmental Skills that I *did master.*

MY *ADULT*

Emotional/Psychological Needs that *were met* by my family:

Love (partially), Guidance (partially)

Psychosocial Developmental Skills that I *mastered:*

Autonomy, Initiative, Industry

ART THERAPY

In the art work that follows, I will show you the progression of my childhood personality structure and the defense mechanisms I used to protect myself. I have drawn a series of children and given them different names, to help me understand myself at various stages of development.

ANNIE

(The drawing of Annie is a reproduction of a painting by Pierre Auguste Renoir; "The Daughters of Catulle Mendes," 1888. My spirit had been attracted to this one little girl, who reminded me of my Annie).

ANNIE

I probably began life like any other baby. I was soft, small, dependent and needy. I cried when I had a need and cried when I was hurt or afraid. I asked my Daddy to carry me. I loved my Mommy. I wanted to please both of them.

I was a girl and was dressed in pretty dresses, given "girl" toys, and amused the people around me with questions and my own special names for things and events. I had a talent for music and art and dancing. I was sensitive, emotional, and aware of events around me. However, at some point in my life with my family I became over-whelmed with what now appear to be traumatic events. I lost all memory prior to age six. I had anxiety attacks, fears and emotional pain. My personality could no longer function as it was. So, this feminine, needy, emotional part of my personality got repressed into my unconscious. It had to be repressed and hidden inside me because it was too painful to experience the emotions of this very "girly girl."

CHARLES PRECIOUS

CHARLES PRECIOUS

Annie became replaced or joined by Charles Precious, around the age of two. I had somehow figured out that being a boy was better, so I decided, on some unconscious level, to become a boy. This part of my personality, however, was not very strong. Charles Precious had the same emotions as Annie and did not do any better handling the emotions. He was an emotional, impotent, frightened boy. When he felt overwhelmed with events in his family or life in general, Charles would "shut down" and escape to his inner world, with his sea-kitty. He would dissociate from the world and dissociate from himself. He could stay stuck there for days at a time.

TOMBOY JUDY

TOMBOY JUDY

I think "Judy" emerged somewhere between the ages of six and ten. I guess some part of me was tired of being a "cry baby" or "impotent little boy," so my personality took a new twist. I became a combination of boy/girl: I took dance lessons, played with girl friends, had a few dolls, and participated in "kissing games." But I also became active and very good in "boys' sports," developed a temper, kicked doors or boys when I was mad.

This part of my personality became my best defense against the world. Tomboy Judy wasn't going to let anyone push me around. She was strong, stubborn, independent, energetic and defiant. Tomboy Judy was the dominant part of my personality, well into adulthood. She hated "girly girls" who giggled and cried and whined. She hated Annie and Charles Precious. She preferred to play with boys, was always tough, and would rather be mad than sad.

After my divorce, this part helped me get through graduate school, but it also terrorized me and my children. Tomboy Judy, herself, was terrorized by blind rage. It cut me off from the sweet, vulnerable, hurting parts of my personality. It prevented me from crying or reaching out. It kept Annie and Charles Precious locked in the "basement" of my unconscious. It kept me from developing the feminine side of my personality.

MY *SELF*

Adult

Needs that were met:
Love (partially)
Guidance (partially)

Skills that I mastered:
Autonomy
Initiative
Industry

Inner Child

Unmet needs:
Love (partially), Approval, Safety, Guidance (partially), Respectful Boundaries and Consequences

Skills I did not master:
Basic Trust, Identity, Intimacy

Childhood Coping Skills:
Repression, idealization, displacement, dissociation, nightmares, high achievement/perfectionism, loss of memory, reaction formation—becoming a "tomboy" and "anti-dependent," rage and altruism

Chapter 8

MY STRUGGLES AS AN ADULT

As I entered adulthood, I was married at age 21 and became a mother the same year. I was a woman who felt more like a boy than a girl, who was poorly equipped to deal with marriage, children or maintaining a home. I had absolutely no clue who I was inside. I had spent a lifetime earning esteem given to me by other people but had really no personal sense of self-worth. As an adolescent, I had never maintained a real job nor had to earn my own money. I had an inner rage that was always at the boiling point and took very little to ignite. I over-reacted to many situations and had a very low frustration tolerance. I had not learned the feminine skills of cooking, sewing or keeping a tidy, clean home.

I married a man who was very domineering and control-ling, hard to please and non-communicative. He made all the decisions, handled all the bills and money. He gave me my "weekly allowance." He was a workaholic who was rarely home and I was living in his country, Canada. I was isolated, lonely, often sad and depressed. By the age of 24, I had my second child and was placed on Valium for one year because I had symptoms of anxiety — constant worrying, fatigue, fear of bad things happening, weight loss, constant crying.

I was devastated when my husband demanded a divorce after only five years of marriage. Even though it was not a healthy relationship, I was deeply in love with him and felt crushed by the rejection. I was 26 years old.

I moved myself and my two children, ages five and two, back to the United States and was in a state of untreated depression, which lasted for a number of years. I used anger and rage to "hold myself together," while I put myself through graduate school and got my first full-time job. I struggled with raising two young children, managing a household on very little income and a small amount of child support. I did not go to counseling because of the family mottos: "Take care of yourself." "Don't talk about bad things." I never talked about my sadness or sense of failure in my marriage, I did not cry. I held all my vulnerable feelings inside myself, like a bottle, and I used anger, like a cork on the bottle, to keep the feelings inside and out of my consciousness. I did not encourage my children to talk about their feelings and losses.

In some ways I was a good mother to my children: I was playful, creative, resourceful, strong, a risk taker, loved them dearly, encouraged them to be athletic, creative, independent, and their own persons. I introduced them to nature and pets. I told them I loved them and gave them lots of time, attention, support and affection. I taught my daughter to cook and sew. I supported all of my sons' athletic activities.

On the other hand, there were ways I failed miserably as a mother. I taught my children that no one could be trusted and that we must take care of ourselves. I taught them not to cry and not to talk about their vulnerable feelings. When I became over-whelmed with pressure, my rage would explode. I set up an environment that was very similar to my own childhood. My young children grew up not feeling safe and holding their feelings inside.

Rage, the defense mechanism of my tomboy *Inner Child*, was clearly maladaptive. It may have helped me survive as a child, but it was harming my children and causing me to hate and loath myself. It frightened me, and I had no way to control it. Blind rage would just explode out of nowhere. I lived with daily fear and shame. I realize now that I could not control my rage because it was a volcano that was fed by the turbulent waters of my unconscious, and I did not know what was in my unconscious. The waters had become toxic from years'-worth of unexpressed, vulnerable emotions. I was a very fragile person with an explosive mixture of emotions trapped inside me and almost any life stress could cause the volcano of rage to erupt.

In terms of dating, I was afraid to be alone with myself and was very codependent in relationships. I often chose partners who were not my equal, so that they would need me and never leave me like my first husband did. I carried my childhood coping mechanisms into adulthood and they prevented me from establishing intimacy with myself and the people I loved.

The defining point in my life happened when I was 33 years old. It was my daughter's eighth birthday and I had taken her, her girlfriend and my son horseback riding. The horse my daughter normally rode was not available, so she was given a horse she had never ridden before. As we rode along, she kept complaining that the horse was too slow. Finally, I decided to let her ride my horse, who was very spirited. She had barely mounted, and I had not had time to adjust the stirrups, when the horse took off in a full gallop and headed back to the barn. I jumped onto the slow horse and tried to catch up with her, but I could only watch in horror as I saw her fall to the ground. When I finally reached her, I saw my baby girl laying face down in the desert dirt, immobile. I ran to her, turned her over and started yelling for help. She was covered with dirt and her head had begun to swell up like a hydrocephalic baby. I was horrified!

In the moments that followed I was in a trance-like state. I made arrangements for the hospital I worked in to be ready to admit her to their emergency department. I drove her across town, talking to her all the way, trying to keep her conscious. Only when she was admitted to the hospital could I collapse in tears. She was diagnosed with a concussion, a broken left leg and a broken right thumb. She had to be in hospital for a week. I get sick in my stomach today as I remember the fear and horror of that day.

When she came home, I took off work and tried the best I could to help her recover from the emotional and physical damage from the fall. We were both over-whelmed. She was angry and frightened, and I was racked with guilt and sadness. The man I was dating at the time broke up with me because he could not deal with the stress. I began to slip into depression.

On one particularly bleak day, I just seemed to "snap." It had been seven years of struggle after my divorce, putting myself through graduate school, then working, raising two small children without any help and very little money, trying to hold things together the best I could, while suffering from my uncontrollable rage — now this frightening accident. Suddenly it was all too much for me to handle. I thought of killing myself. Then I thought that if I killed myself, I could not leave my children alone, I would have to kill them, too! As soon as that thought came to my mind, I knew I would never do it, but I realized what bad shape I was in.

For the first time in my life, my defense system was not working. I realized that I needed help. I called out to God to help me. I had gone through life defiantly independent and self-willed. I had been in a tug-of-war with God and now I was ready to admit defeat. I cried out to God and invited Him to enter my life and help me. Without even knowing it, I had worked the first three steps in the Twelve-Step program.

My life changed dramatically from that day on. Through daily prayer and journaling, I began to pour out the depths of pain in my heart, releasing the years'-worth of unexpressed fear, anguish and vulnerability. For the first time in my life, I released the contents of my unconscious. I allowed the feelings I had dissociated from my whole life, that I had stored in the basement of my unconscious, to enter my body. And I felt their full ferocity. I felt the tremendous pain and anxiety I had run from as a child. I was flooded with memories and painful events from my earlier life. I wrote about them and cried about them. I released the energy of their sting from my body, and God filled me with peace.

At the same time, God began to speak to me through random scripture verses and gave me guidance and direction from the Spirit. I was led to read certain books, begin therapy and move to Los Angeles, for further study. I easily found a job and a home in Santa Monica, which has been my "base" for thirty-three years. From then on, He has been healing, transforming and teaching me every day. He has led me through the remaining steps in the Twelve-Step program. The greatest wisdom I have acquired has been from God, teaching me in the privacy of my own home. He has been my teacher, my friend, my therapist, my Father, my guide. There is no more rage living inside me.

Chapter 9

LEARNING NEW RULES TO LIVE BY

Over the last thirty-three years, I have acquired healthier coping mechanisms and a great deal of first-hand knowledge about inner healing, both in my life and in the lives of my clients. My Inner Children have been revealed to me through my dreams and have been released from their bondage. They have brought softness and vulnerability and love, creativity and joy into my life. I have shared my healing and transformation with my children and they have enjoyed a better two decades of their lives. We are able to talk on a deep, intimate level about our feelings, and they are beginning to emerge as healthier adults in their own lives. They are both married to spouses who love them, who have enriched our family. Each of my children has blessed me with a precious grandchild; I have one boy and one girl.

I had a brief second marriage. The man I married was more of a companion than a husband. I was not ready for true intimacy at that time, nor was he. We mutually decided to divorce after three years. That relationship brought a temporary respite to my loneliness and gave me the courage to do the necessary work to prepare myself for a healthier marriage.

After years of hard work on my *Self*, I was finally ready for a healthy marriage and true intimacy. I believe it was God who brought my husband and I together. We have been married for sixteen years, and I can honestly say that I love my husband more with each passing year. I thank God for the gift of our marriage, for giving me my heart's desire. At last, I know what it means to be truly loved and cherished.

I was originally drawn into the helping profession because I unconsciously wanted to give people the love and help I could not give myself. By God's grace and the irony of the spiritual laws of the Universe, it was by helping others that I, in turn, learned to help and love myself. Through the power of God working in my life, combined with individual therapy and work with my husband and children, I am acquiring the psychosocial developmental skills I had not mastered in my family of origin: trust (of *Self* and others), identity and intimacy. I am learning to provide for my five Emotional/Psychological needs: love, approval, safety, guidance, and respectful boundaries and consequences and to provide for the needs of the people I love. Please notice that I said, "I am acquiring," "I am learning." Healing and growth are an on-going process.

As a healthy adult, I have written new, functional rules that I live by:

♦ *"It's okay to make mistakes and to admit it when I do."*

♦ *"I don't have to be perfect and don't even want to be."*

♦ *"It's wise and good to ask for help when I need it."*

♦ *"Certain people can be trusted. Trust must be earned over time, by consistent behavior."*

♦ *"God loves me and is always there to help and guide me."*

♦ *"It's beautiful to be a woman and men have beauty, too."*

♦ *"Vulnerability is a necessary ingredient in a loving relationship with the Self and others. I can be vulnerable and set boundaries and limits with others, so that they do not take advantage of my weakness."*

♦ *"When I do something wrong, I take responsibility for my wrong doing, ask forgiveness and seek to improve my behavior."*

♦ *"It is good to be connected to my body, mind, emotions and spirit."*

♦ *"It is good to speak the truth from my heart."*

♦ *"Love and sex is a good thing."*

♦ *"Men and women can have good, functional relationships and marriages."*

♦ *"The needs and wants of children are as important as the needs and wants of parents."*

♦ *"I love myself and see myself as a pretty, special person worthy of love, happiness, health, abundance and power in my environment."*

♦ *"It is good to express my wants and needs directly. If others can't or won't help me, I can provide for myself."*

♦ *"The spiritual laws of the Universe respond to my thoughts and actions to bring good things and good people into my life."*

> ♦ *"My wealth is defined by the love I give and receive from my family, friends and clients."*
>
> ♦ *"I choose to be the "Survivor/Conqueror," rather than the "Helpless Victim" when faced with the obstacles that life throws at me."*

JUDITH ANNE

JUDITH ANNE

Judith Anne is the healthy, "*functional Adult*" part of my person-ality who has emerged through years of healing. She is the loving mother who has moved into my inner house to take care of my Inner Children. She is here to love them, teach and guide them, help them feel safe and keep them in line.

It was her job to tell Tomboy Judy that she could no longer run the house and terrorize the children. It was her job to bring Annie and Charles Precious out of the basement. It was her job to take all the children in her arms and rock them, sing to them and let them know that they are loved and safe at last. The basement door to my unconscious has been unlocked and they are all free to roam around the house and play.

We all live together in Light, Laughter and Love. When threatening events occur, the children tell me their feelings and their needs and I provide for them. They, in turn, give me spontaneity, joy, energy, creativity and intimacy on a very deep level. Because we are at peace in my inner house, I am free to love and nurture and risk and create in the outer world. At last, I am "comfortable in my own skin."

EXPANDED ART WORK

As a result of my "integrated inner personalities," I am experiencing a renaissance of creative pursuits: I am writing…, sewing…, drawing…, decorating…, gardening…, making jewelry…, finding new ways to express my spirit every day.

TRANSFORMATION OF MY *SELF*
INTEGRATION OF *ADULT*/INNER CHILDREN

With Transformation and Integration,
the *Adult* and Inner Children become one *Self:*
overlapping, accessible to one another

Chapter 10

EXAMPLES OF "SELF-HELP" TOOLS

I will conclude this section by sharing some examples of "self-help tools" — dream analysis and creative writing — which you can use to understand yourself and your own process of development. The story that follows was derived from a section of a dream and a creative writing I did. This writing helped me understand some of the defense mechanisms I developed in childhood which I may have a tendency to use even today, if I am faced with overwhelming stress.

The character in the dream (Charles Precious pictured on page 110) was a gifted, autistic boy who loved to play in the water with his kitten, who is a "sea-kitty" who has skin like a fish and loves the water, but is actually a unique cat from the feline species. He is playful, darling and loves the water. I took the image of the boy and did a "creative writing" about him, where one would take the image and just start writing.

CREATIVE WRITING

Charles Precious Story

"The autistic boy was a very special, gifted, but frightened boy who hid his treasures within the safe labyrinths of his inner recesses. Somehow, early in his life, he learned that the world was not a safe place. On the contrary, the world was a place where you could get "zapped" and hurt if you walked or talked or breathed without your shield of protection. It was a world that could easily hurt the heart and feelings of a sensitive little boy.

So, being a clever little boy, he learned to hide all his wonderful feelings and to tuck them in the pools of his unconscious. They had to go in the unconscious, because if he, himself, felt them he would be overwhelmed with the pain and the sadness. He became very, very clever indeed, snatching his feelings and his dreams and his creative gifts. Snatching them from detection and hiding his wonderful secrets deep inside, in the great pool of the unconscious.

That's why he loved the water so much. That's why he was always frolicking in the water with his darling sea-kitty, because that's the only place in the universe where he could merge with his greater *Self*.

Elsewhere, he was a frightened, impotent and a self-conscious little being. He could not talk to his mother, who was always hovering nearby. She never understood him and was often critical. She hated when he withheld his words or wore "that look" on his face. The look was often fear and pain and she sure didn't want to see that. No indeed! She always told him to wear a smile. She didn't care if it was a phony smile, a plastic smile or a nothing smile. She didn't care what price he paid when he tried to smile for her, tried to please her.

So the little boy did the best he could. He hid deep inside himself. He avoided people because he was leery of them. He was a prisoner in his own little cocoon. He couldn't reach out or embrace his many wonderful parts because he was so afraid and fragile. He had never experienced true acceptance.

Life seemed dangerous. Was he not dangerous too? To breathe is to expand and feel and express and expose, to reveal and be seen and to experience. So mostly he just held his breath and tried to be invisible. "If I'm little and small and quiet and still, no one will see me and no one will squish me. If I'm in a crowd and I sit on the outskirts, keeping very quiet and watching... watching... watching... I can spot danger and be ready to run. I dare not open my mouth, because then they'll see me and then they can get me. When I walk in a crowd I'll keep a protective cocoon of air around me. I'll get everything I need from my own little cocoon: air, space, protection, privacy, a place where I can hide. It will keep bad vibes from touching me and will contain my own vibes. I'll be safe and alone."

ALONE... always alone. *I am* the boy in the plastic bubble. The boy who looks out at the world but never connects. The boy who wants to play, break out and break through. The boy who wants friends with whom to rough house, kiss and hug him. The boy who wants to run to mother's welcoming arms. The boy who wants to cry his heart out, have someone put a band aide on and make it all better. The boy who is lonely and lost and trapped in his plastic bubble... The boy who trusts no one. The boy who aches to be liked and loved. The boy who feels ugly and wretched. The boy who wants a friend. Will you be my friend? The boy who is scared of the dark. The boy who lives in the dark. The boy who is really a *girl* but doesn't even know it. "Won't you love me? Won't you care for me? Won't you take me out of this bubble?"

(An interesting side note is that as a young child, as early as age two, I referred to myself as "Charles," even though my name was Judith Anne or Judy. This may have been influenced by the fact that we had three or four bachelor officers living in our home at the time. My mother, then, would call me "Precious Charles," which over the years got converted to "Charles Precious" as my nickname.)

DREAM ANALYSIS

I never worked with the image of the "sea-kitty" until I was just now typing this dream into my computer. I found the image rather fascinating and decided I would now work with it in a "Jungian" way. Carl Gustav Jung, the prominent Swiss psychiatrist who founded the school of analytical psychology, was fascinated with the unconscious, dreams, spirituality and healing. He had the theory that dreams are the pathway to the unconscious and that every image in a dream is part of the dreamer and reflects a message about the dreamer's personality. So, let's see what that sea-kitty tells me about myself. To do this, I'll write down the characteristics I associate with the kitten:

- The kitten in general – small, lively, playful, independent nature, full of life, happy, fearless, spontaneous, amuses itself with the simplest of things.

- This special species of "sea-kitty" has outer scales on the body to protect the vulnerable inner skin, lives in the water, loves to play with the autistic boy, is both a warm blooded and cold blooded creature, is specially adapted to breathe under water.

- The water – In Jungian dream work, the water is often seen as a symbol of the unconscious.

The message from the symbol of the sea-kitty seems to be that I have all the qualities of the kitten living deep inside me, in my unconscious. If I want to enrich my life in the outer world, I have to "take off the scales from my outer body" which I have used, like armor, to protect myself psychologically all these years.

I will have to confront the repressed part of me that is both warm blooded (able to feel, to be warm, to bond) and the cold blooded part of me (that which is cold, distant, "non human," dissociated). I have to take the kitten out of my unconscious and let its good qualities manifest themselves in my outer life. I have to risk being playful, spontaneous, full of life, happy, fearless. I have to take pleasure in the simple things in life. I can still have my independent nature, but I have to learn to play with others.

SECTION THREE

SELECTING THE BEST POSSIBLE MATE

*"In order to choose someone who 'fits' you,
you must first know who you are."*

~ J.D.

Chapter 11

EXAMINE YOUR MOTIVES FOR WANTING LOVE AND MARRIAGE

*"Are you seeking someone to 'fix' you
or save you from yourself?"*

~J.D.

Section One was all about preparing yourself to be the best possible mate. This chapter will investigate your motives and readiness for a relationship

Before we dive into this chapter I want you to do some thinking. At this point in your life, are you happy with yourself, capable of taking care of your basic needs and wants? In deciding you want to marry, are you looking for a mate whom you can love, share life and dreams with and enhance the good life you already have? If you answered both questions "Yes," I would say that you want to get married for healthy reasons.

If you are not happy with yourself and are not yet capable of taking care of your basic wants and needs, I would advise you to stop the search for a marriage partner and concentrate on preparing yourself for the marriage you want to have someday. Right now, you should spend time making a life for yourself that is full and meaningful. There are many facets of your life to be explored:

- Have you completed your education?
- Do you have a job that utilizes your abilities and gives you satisfaction?
- Are you able to provide for yourself financially?
- Do you have a social life, hobbies, interests, passions?
- Are you able to spend time by yourself and not feel frightened or lonely?
- Are you connected to your community?
- Are you connected to your family?
- Do you have friends with whom you are intimate?
- Do you take care of your own body, mind, emotions and spirit?
- Do you know what your values are?
- What are your goals in life?
- What do you know about your present emotional life and the life of your unconscious?

Indeed, being around others, in school, on the job, dating, in activities, in the community all help us understand who we are, what we need and what we want. If you have led a fairly isolated life up to this point, I would advise you to "get a life" before searching for someone to marry. Only when you know and understand yourself will you be able to pick someone who will be a good mate for you.

TIPS FOR DATING

If you don't have much experience with dating, whether due to a poor self-image, shyness or lack of opportunity, here are some pointers to help you along the way:

♦ **First, you have to believe that you are "worthy" of dating and having fun.** There are some spiritual laws which come into play in our lives and you need to be aware of them: **The Universe will only give you things when you are ready to receive them.**

♦ **You must be specific about what you want.** If you aim for nothing, that is what you get. You must first have the thought, the goal clearly established in your mind and heart. This will seep down into your unconscious and your body, so that every part of you is in agreement about your goal. By doing this, you will generate positive energy into the Universe and God, people, serendipitous events, your own intuition and the Universe will assist in bringing to you that which you seek.

♦ **You have to let people know that you are "open" to dating.** Many times, when people feel poorly about themselves, they don't make eye contact and their body language is closed off (head down, arms crossed, walking too fast, absorbed in their own thoughts). Or, they stay "holed up" in their homes, lamenting that they never meet anyone to date. Or, they project their own feelings of insecurity onto other people (i.e. "No one will be interested in me because I am too _____, _____, etc.).

♦ **You need to practice making eye contact and having conversations with people you see,** and let yourself gather "data" from them about their feelings about you. Do they smile? Do they try to make conversation with you? Do they seem interested in you? Do they make excuses to be around you? Odds are there are people who are interested in you. You must give them permission to "come into your space" and invite you out. By making eye contact, opening up your body language, and making conversation, you will let people know that you are "open for contact."

♦ **There are other ways to become "proactive" on your own behalf:** You need to get out of your house and get involved in special interests. You will often meet people who have similar interests. You need to accept invitations to social events, even when you don't feel like going. You need to let family and friends know that you are interested in dating. You can experiment with "singles events." If you feel unattractive, you can begin to work out and exercise, eat healthier, buy attractive new clothes in brighter colors, try a new hair style, go for massage and other types of body care.

♦ **It's good to date a variety of people.** Sometimes, we don't know ourselves or our worth as of yet, and the people we date can help us learn and expand ourselves. **Each person you date is a potential "teacher."** Sometimes the lessons we learn are good and sometimes they are bad. You will find that some people treat you with respect and that many others do not. You will find that some dates are attractive to you on many different levels, and some are not attractive on any level. You will find that you desire to spend a lot of time with some dates while others, you don't wish to see more than once. The important thing is to learn the inherent lessons. By dating a variety of people, we are exposed to many ideas, cultures, values and experiences. Each person teaches us something about our *Self*.

♦ **Sometimes we do not know that we have "worth" until someone treats us badly,** and we realize that the experience hurt or disappointed us. Sometimes we have to be treated badly over and over, until we finally reach a point where we say "No more. I am worth more than that."

♦ **Sometimes we choose a person who does not match us in terms of intelligence, ambition, life style or values.** We make excuses for the person, or try to change them to become more like us, or we tell ourselves that the "miss-match" doesn't really matter because we love them, are infatuated with them or are afraid of being alone until the "right" person comes along. When this happens, we may have to invest a lot of time and emotion into the relation-ship, only to find out, in the end, that the relationship is not really what we want or need. This is how we learn about ourselves. "I have learned more about what I must have in a relationship and, in doing so, I have learned more about myself."

♦ **Sometimes we let a person try to change us into their image of what and who we should be:** We lose weight, dye our hair, wear the clothes they suggest, talk, think, and act more like them — all in an attempt to please them and have them like us. At times, we are happy with our "new self," but, often, we realize that it just doesn't work. We have lost our uniqueness, our individual spirit, our essence. We have pleased someone else, indulged their fantasy, but have lost our *Self*. In this case, we have to leave the person or hope they can accept who we really are. "I found out who I am, by finding out who I am *not*."

♦ **Keep in mind that every dating situation has a 50-50 percent chance of success and failure.** That is the nature of dating. You must be ready to risk liking someone and being rejected. The other person takes the same risk. The important thing here is to be honest and give a full disclosure about your intentions. If you just want to date and don't plan to get involved, say so. If you want to date several people at the same time, say so. If you want to have sex, but don't want to get emotionally involved, say so. If you are really looking for a relationship, say so. There's no sense wasting the other person's time or having them waste yours. You might be rejected. Or you may end up achieving your goals. If you don't get what you want with this person, then you must press on. Remember: ultimately, you will get what you want.

♦ **Sometimes people are thwarted in the dating arena because they have an over-inflated idea of their own desirability.** *You have to be realistic about who you are and whom you can attract*. This seems to be especially true of some men, whereas women seem more likely to undervalue themselves, based on societal emphasis on being "pretty, thin, blonde, buxom," etc.

Take, for instance, the man who is over-weight, average to low income, average education, poor dresser, average car, sloppy eater and poor manners. He is not likely to attract the "10" woman he is adamant about dating. He would be much better advised to date women who are more "average" like he is, although he denies this quality himself.

Then, there is the gorgeous guy who has no job or transportation. He might get picked up as a "boy toy," but he won't be perceived as "husband material."

There are some cruel hard facts which seem to exist in the dating world:

♦ **Men often choose "good looks"** as their first requirement for dating and are less concerned about the woman's income, job and education. Men want a woman who is sexually appealing.

♦ **Women who are looking for a marriage partner** are most often looking for a man with a certain amount of power and an income, which will provide a home and financial security. Women also want good personality traits and are less concerned with great looks, although few women would turn away a man who is good looking and has the above characteristics.

DYSFUNCTIONAL DATING

Generally, the more dysfunctional your family of origin, the more dysfunctional you are likely to be. Some examples of "dysfunctional dating" are:

- Physically, emotionally or sexually abusive relationships.

- Dating emotionally unavailable people. (You get attached, but they don't)

- Dating people who don't "match" your values and goals.
- Dating people who "use" you for financial or emotional gain, and give nothing in return.
- Dating people you would be embarrassed to introduce to your family.
- Dating "flakey," unreliable people. (last minute cancellations, no shows, no apologies)
- Dating only people who look like a past rejecting lover in an attempt to replace the loss.
- Dating people who are substitute "mothers" and "fathers."
- Dating people who are only interested in exploiting you sexually.
- Using people for your own purposes and then casually dumping them.

Chapter 12

PERSONAL INVENTORY

*"Self-knowledge is an invaluable asset. What are your needs,
values, goals, abilities and weaknesses?"*

~ J.D.

To assist you in understanding yourself and your current level of functioning, I have prepared the following Questionnaire. Copy the questions and answer them in detail.

1. What did you learn about YOURSELF from your past relationships?

2. How do you make yourself happy?

3. What makes you unhappy or sad?

4. Are you able to communicate your feelings/needs directly?

5. How do you handle anger?

6. How do you handle conflict?

7. How do you handle stress?

8. How do you handle hurt/disappointment?

9. How do you handle sadness?

10. How do you handle fear?

11. Are you able to set "respectful boundaries and limits" with people?

12. Do you have a personal belief in God? Explain it.

13. Do you put barriers between yourself and other people? Explain...

14. What is your style for solving problems?

15. Are you able to establish emotional intimacy with other people?

16. Do you feel frightened, lonely or bored when you are alone with yourself? Do you distract yourself with noise or "busyness"?

17. Are you able to admit when you are wrong or have made a mistake?

18. Are you able to give or ask for forgiveness?

19. How do you feel about sex? Can you talk openly about it with partners? What you want? What you don't want? Are you the initiator or the passive one in your sexual relationship? What form of birth control do you use?

20. Describe your current relationship with your family of origin (mother, father, siblings).

21. What are your "pet peeves" around the house?

22. What is your fighting style: silence..., loud and scary..., name calling..., vulgarities..., hit below the belt..., sarcasm..., violence..., try to fight fair..., passive-aggressive..., run away..., assertive..., crying...?

23. What are your eating habits (health foods, junk/fast foods, snacker, over-eat when upset, under-eat when upset, or pretty well balanced)?

24. Describe your exercise program.

25. Describe your personal values and life goals.

26. Describe your strengths and weaknesses.

27. How do you handle your bills and financial obligations? Do you pay your bills on time? Do you have money in savings? Do you have credit card debt? Have you declared bankruptcy?

28. Are you currently indulging in food, alcohol or substance abuse or other addictive, mood altering behaviors

(obsessive shopping, gambling, sex, etc.)? If so, have you ever been in treatment or considered it?

29. Are you currently suffering from a single or multiple episodes of a mood disorder? If so, have you ever been treated with psychiatric medication or psychotherapy?

30. Are there any areas of your life where you are "of service" to others? Such as pets, children, parents, organizations, volunteering, mentoring, donations?

ANALYSIS OF YOUR CURRENT LEVEL OF FUNCTIONING

On a scale of 1 (least healthy) to 10 (most healthy), evaluate how well you are taking care of yourself.

1 · · · · · · · · 3 · · · · · · · · 5 · · · · · · · · 7 · · · · · · 10

   a.   Are you taking care of your body, mind, emotions and spirit?

   b.   Are you providing yourself with love, approval, safety, guidance and respectful boundaries and consequences?

c. Do you have wounded Inner Children who are running the show?

d. Are you acting in a responsible way in terms of your life and the lives of others?

If you rated your functionality with a high number, your life sounds pretty healthy and balanced. You have a high degree of healthy adult and healthy Inner Child operating in your life. The odds are that you will attract a healthy mate.

If your self assessment reveals a low number, it is safe to say that your dysfunctional Inner Child is running your life. Take a serious pause here and think about what I said in Section One, Chapter 5: "A Holistic Commitment to Your *Self.*" Remember, that if you are operating in dysfunction (as opposed to health), you will attract a dysfunctional mate.

Chapter 13

REVIEW OF SIGNIFICANT PAST RELATIONSHIPS

*"Sometimes we find out who we ARE by finding out who we
are NOT. Unsuccessful past relationships can tell us a lot
about our own functioning and about
our level of self-awareness at the time."*

~ J.D.

To assist you in evaluating yourself and your past relationships, I developed the following Questionnaire. Use this Questionnaire to assess each of your most significant past relationships. Copy the questions and answer them in detail.

REVIEW OF SIGNIFICANT PAST RELATIONSHIPS QUESTIONNAIRE

1. How did you meet this person?

2. What did they do for a living?

3. What originally attracted you to this person?

4. What information did this person give you early on — information you heard, but didn't want to hear and which eventually "bit you in the ass" at the end of the relationship?

5. When you first met this person, what level of relationship did *they* reveal they were looking for?

6. When you first met this person, what level of relationship were *you* looking for?

7. Describe the communication style of this person.

8. Describe how this person dealt with anger and conflicts.

9. How open was this person about prior relationships?

10. If the other person was open about prior relationships, what seemed to be the major issues which ended those relationships?

11. What did you have in common with this person? Interests, activities, religion, children, etc.

12. Describe how this person handled financial matters in regard to dating, joint activities, gifts, debt, monthly expenses.

13. If you lived with this person, how did you handle the division of joint financial obligations?

14. What did you have in common with this person in regard to values and level of spiritual development?

15. What did you learn about this person and their family of origin? How did they get along with their mother, father, siblings?

16. At what point in the relationship did the "C" and "M" words (commitment and marriage) come up and who originated them?

17. Describe the event during which the relationship first appeared to begin to dissolve. (the point at which you became disenchanted).

18. What were the things you initially wanted to change about this person?

19. What were the things they initially wanted to change about you?

20. How quickly did you get sexually involved, who initiated it and did you practice safe sex?

21. What were the major areas of contention in the relationship?

22. What was the "deal breaker" in the relationship?

23. How did YOU operate within the relationship? (in terms of power, assertiveness, getting your needs met, expressing yourself, handling anger and conflict).

24. Did you feel safe, valued, respected in the relationship?

25. Was this person able to establish emotional intimacy?

26. Did you have any pets or children and how did this person interact with them?

27. Did this person have any pets or children and how did you interact with them?

28. How did this person interact with their own pets or children?

29. Rate this person according to the following "CHARACTER TYPES." Copy and circle the ones that apply to them.
  - ☐ "FIXER-UPPER"
  - ☐ "TOO-SLICK; TOO GOOD TO BELIEVE"
  - ☐ "HIGH MAINTENANCE"
  - ☐ "DON JUAN/WOMAN 10"
  - ☐ "FATHER/MOTHER"
  - ☐ "PETER PAN/PRINCESS"
  - ☐ "BAD BOY/BAD GIRL"
  - ☐ "UNAVAILABLE"
  - ☐ "CONTROLLER"
  - ☐ "VICTIM"
  - ☐ "SOMEONE TO PLAY WITH"
  - ☐ "STABLE BOY/GIRL NEXT DOOR"
  - ☐ "EXPLOSIVE, SHORT FUSE"
  - ☐ "SHAMER"
  - ☐ "NURTURER"
  - ☐ "TAKER"
  - ☐ "CONTROLLED, PEOPLE PLEASER"

30. Rate yourself according to the following "CHARACTER TYPES." Copy and circle the ones that applied to you in this relationship.
  - ☐ "FIXER-UPPER"
  - ☐ "TOO SLICK-TOO GOOD TO BELIEVE"
  - ☐ "HIGH MAINTENANCE"
  - ☐ "DON JUAN/ WOMAN 10"
  - ☐ "FATHER/ MOTHER"
  - ☐ "PETER PAN/ PRINCESS"
  - ☐ "BAD BOY/ BAD GIRL"

- ☐ "UNAVAILABLE"
- ☐ "CONTROLLER"
- ☐ "VICTIM"
- ☐ "SOMEONE TO PLAY WITH"
- ☐ "STABLE BOY/ GIRL NEXT DOOR"
- ☐ "EXPLOSIVE, SHORT FUSE"
- ☐ "SHAMER"
- ☐ "NURTURER"
- ☐ "TAKER"
- ☐ "CONTROLLED, PEOPLE PLEASER"

Chapter 14

PARTNER "WISH LIST"
Romantic Qualities vs.
Characteristics of the Spirit

*"Many times Hollywood's version of the
perfect mate will not withstand the pressures
and strains of marriage and life."*

~ J.D.

I often encourage clients to begin making a "wish list" of qualities they want their mate to have. I give them the example of shopping for a book on Amazon.com: "When you are browsing on Amazon.com, you scan various titles of books or categories of books, and then you "click" on them to get more information. You gather as much data as you can and when you find one that really interests you, you "put it in the shopping cart" and have it sent to your home. Once you get it, if you don't like it, you can return it to Amazon and get your money back.

In the proceeding chapter, I gave you the opportunity to analyze your past significant relationships. If you have done enough dating and are now sure that you want to move toward selecting a marriage partner, it's best to begin by constructing a PARTNER "WISH LIST." What I am asking you to do may seem tedious, but I assure you it is one of THE MOST IMPORTANT steps you will ever take toward providing yourself with a healthy, successful marriage. Keep in mind that this LIST is not intended to be completed in one sitting. It is easily something which could takes months to complete or could even be completed in sections, at your leisure.

INITIAL PARTNER "WISH LIST"

Think carefully about what qualities and attributes you want your mate to have and jot them down on an INITIAL LIST in your journal or in the workbook.

POSITIVE QUALITIES FROM PAST RELATIONSHIPS

To augment this INITIAL LIST, I want you to complete some additional information.

Analyze the qualities you liked about every significant person you have dated and add them to the LIST. You should also add to this list any qualities which you now realize you must have in a mate. These might reflect areas where you have grown as a person or have a better understanding of who you are and what you need in a mate.

MY PERSONAL QUALITIES, VALUES AND LIFE GOALS

Next, I want you to write down the key qualities, strengths, weakness, values and goals which describe you. This will help you be aware of exactly who you are and what type of mate you'll need to "match" you. I am a firm believer that the more you have in common with a mate, the closer your compatibility and the easier your adjustment will be. You may have heard that opposites attract, but the truth is that, often, they will eventually repel each other.

TRAITS IN MY PARTNER THAT WILL HELP "ROUND ME OUT"

Once you have completed your List about your *Self*, go through it and circle the most important qualities, values and goals that you would like your future mate to match. Next, go through and identify your "weak points" and circle them. These will help you be aware of traits you will want your mate to have, because it might help "balance out" your weaknesses or short comings. For instance, an introvert might do well with a mate who is more extroverted. A person who is poor with money management might do well with someone who is good at finances and budgets. A person who is "high strung," might do well with a mate who is patient and "low-key." This is one area where it is good to have some differences and where you can actually learn and expand from exposure to the other person.

PARTNER "CHARACTERISTICS OF THE SPIRIT" LIST

Finally, I will suggest some attributes you might add to your PARTNER "WISH LIST."

What I mean by "Characteristics of the Spirit" are **the inner qualities of the person which reflect the heart, the values, the psychological coping mechanisms and the spiritual aspect of the person.** These are qualities which are not easily observed and evident. They are not like external aspects of the person (looks, job, education, income, sex appeal, etc.) which reveal themselves pretty quickly.

To learn about his or her characteristics of the spirit, you must spend a great deal of time with the person and observe their behavior over time. You will learn these qualities after six months or more, when the "first blush" of the relationship has worn off and the underlying qualities emerge.

I cannot stress how important these qualities are for a healthy long-term relationship and marriage. They are often what determine if the symbolic "house" of the relationship can survive in the storms of life. Many people pick a marriage partner with excellent external characteristics, only to find out in the course of the marriage that this same partner lacks the spiritual character traits required for a successful marriage. They are heart broken when the partner cannot give them what they need and want.

ATTRIBUTES OF "CHARACTERISTICS OF THE SPIRIT"

- wants to be in a committed relationship or marriage
- takes responsibility for personal growth
- takes responsibility of own *Self* (body, mind, emotions, spirit)

- uses self-discipline — is able to postpone instant gratification
- treats you with respect
- makes you feel valuable and safe
- has flexible, personal boundaries and respects your boundaries
- is capable of emotional, physical and sexual intimacy
- is able to communicate and listen to and respect what you have to say
- has problem solving skills
- has frustration tolerance
- deals with anger in a healthy, constructive manner
- believes in some sort of "Higher Power" and "service" to mankind
- is able to admit mistakes
- is able to ask for and give forgiveness
- encourages and supports your highest growth
- is independent, yet capable of "interdependence"

This List is only a sample, meant to stimulate your own thoughts. Of course you can make your own List, based on your inner values and personal awareness of what you want. The important thing is that you have some list of INNER QUALITIES AND STRENGTHS identified which you think are important for maintaining a relationship and a marriage.

All too often people pick a mate based on "externals" which look good, only to find out the person does not have the inner qualities required to carry through with a relationship. And a marriage is much more complicated than a mere relationship.

A marriage will involve many decades of life and additional people (children, in-laws and other family members, etc.). Each decade of life will bring new stressors and challenges. Only those marriages with a strong internal foundation will survive.

By this time, you have completed an extensive number of LISTS:

- INITIAL PARTNER "WISH LIST"

- POSITIVE QUALITIES FROM PAST RELATIONSHIPS

- MY PERSONAL QUALITIES, VALUES AND LIFE GOALS

- TRAITS IN MY PARTNER THAT WILL HELP "ROUND ME OUT"

- PARTNER "CHARACTERISTICS OF THE SPIRIT" LIST

You are now ready to compile one COMPLETED PARTNER "WISH LIST." To do this, take a separate sheet of paper and consolidate or list your attributes and wishes from the five lists you've just completed.

Once you have compiled your list, you are ready for the next step in the process of finding your ideal mate. This step involves making a conscious COMMITMENT to your COMPLETED PARTNER "WISH LIST." You must be clear that you will not settle for a marriage partner who does not possess the most important qualities on your list. Go through your List and circle the qualities which you simply MUST have. The ones that remain will be seen as of secondary importance and not essential.

I think it is fair to say that we rarely get every single criterion on our LIST. That is nearly impossible. Sometimes we have to accept some "trade offs." For instance, a person who wants to have children, who falls in love with someone who meets most of their criteria, but is unable, through infertility, tubal ligation, hysterectomy or vasectomy, to have children. A tall person who wants a tall mate, but falls in love with the person who comes in a 5'4" package. Or finding the "perfect mate" who comes wrapped in an ethnic or religious package they had not expected.

The qualities you circle become your "yard stick" or template for evaluating all future dates as your possible marriage partner. You have passed the point of no return of "carefree dating." Because you are clear that you want to get married, you have to become a "serious shopper." You have to feel that you are entitled to gather enough information to determine if this person has potential to be a marriage partner. That means you have to feel comfortable asking pertinent questions. You also have to listen closely to the answers you get. You must be serious enough about your endeavor to find the right mate to know, if the person does not meet the criteria on your list, you will not waste your time. You will not continue to see that person if they are not qualified. You must see this process very much like interviewing someone for a job or like comparison shopping. You will only accept the best person for the job or the best product.

I suggest that on every first date, you take an active role in gathering information and data about the person. Ask a lot of questions and listen closely to what they tell you about themselves. Pay very close attention! On first dates people are often very chatty and will volunteer lots of information about themselves. And they tend to tell the truth.

Listen closely to what they say about past relationships and why the relationships ended. Pay attention to what were the complaints about them from past partners. You can gather a WEALTH of valuable information. The first date is an excellent time to do it because you are not yet involved with the person and can be more objective. Once you become sexually involved, you will be much less objective and will tend to disregard, minimize or deny information that you don't want to hear.

SECTION FOUR

Working Together to Achieve a Healthy Relationship

"A healthy friendship is the best guarantee of a healthy marriage."

~ J.D.

Understanding the Phases of Growth to Creating a Healthy Relationship and Marriage

In an attempt to save you heartache and guide you in the process of establishing a healthy relationship and a healthy marriage, I am going to present a model of the various phases you must pass through and make certain recommendations for each phase.

Chapter 15

INTRODUCTION TO THE DATING PHASE

"The tip of the iceberg is not dangerous because it can be easily seen. It is the **base** *of the iceberg, hidden below the surface of the water, which sinks ships."*

~ J.D.

In this chapter, let's assume that you have just met "Mr. or Ms. Right." Naturally, after all the personal work you did on yourself and all the tedious work of screening potential candidates, your hormones are jumping and you are anxious to plunge directly into the relationship. On the very first date you are so excited and so enamored with the person of your dreams that you want to have sex right away. You might be saying, "I know this is the right one for me. I can just feel it. I don't want to wait to have sex. I want to do it right away."

I have seen this scenario over and over again with my clients. They may have been in therapy with me for six months to a year, working on healing their Inner Child and strengthening their healthy coping skills, yet, in one night of Kismet, everything we have been working on goes right out the window, and their Inner Child takes over. Instead of just having a nice date and saying "Goodbye" at the door, the Inner Child sets a "web of seduction" where the new date is invited in, ostensibly for a night cap, a cup of coffee, a dip in the hot tub, etc., and they end up in the bedroom, making love with a total stranger. **Instant intimacy!**

We have all been there, done that. Generally, it is the earmark of a poor beginning. What happens in these cases is that your Inner Child has put you in psychological danger. The Inner Child is all about instant gratification, immediacy, trusting only that which can be seen in the moment. The Inner Child sees something it wants and wants to have the FULL experience RIGHT NOW! To the child, there is no waiting, no tomorrow, no postponement.

The reason I say your Inner Child has put you in psychological danger is that, in the above scenario, you have let a total stranger penetrate your most intimate physical parts without having established one ounce of trust. You have literally invited this stranger into your body and your psyche, all in the name of "being attracted," "falling in love on the first date."

All of this flies in opposition to the way we establish intimacy with most of the people we know. Generally, it takes us **years** to establish trust with parents, siblings, friends or co-workers. The trust is established slowly, through gradual increments, consistent behavior and ever deepening levels. And in all these relationships, except in the case of a baby with his or her parents, we would never think of exposing our nude bodies on a first meeting.

Why then do we "lose our heads" on a first date, jumping in with both feet and no logic? The answer is that your Inner Child has run the show, not your adult. And what generally happens is that your adult part or the adult part of the other person gets scared after the instant intimacy. The adult part of you is, by nature, less trusting. It might say to you the morning after, "Oh my God. What have I done? Why on earth did I do that? What am I going to do now? I don't even know that person and, yet, I've already had sex." Many times, one or the other of you will retreat, either from fear or from having "made the conquest" too soon. It might not happen right away, but it might happen after a few more dates.

Another possibility is that you will spend too much time together too soon, only to find the relationship burns out quickly. Or, the woman may feel she had sex too soon and on subsequent dates she tells the man that she wants to "slow down and get to know you better." The man, who had the enjoyment of sex on the very first date, is forced to "back track." He may then feel confused, frustrated and angry. Another possibility is that the man who had sex on the first date may become afraid that the woman will expect a commitment because of having sex with him. This could cause him to run away. In most of these cases, what might have been a good relationship is doomed before it even gets off the ground.

Chapter 16

DATING PHASE

What I am going to tell you about this first phase of your potential relationship is the same thing I tell my clients: Proceed SLOWLY. Just as it took you a long time to get to know yourself; it will take a long time to get to know this new person of your dreams. There is no such thing as "instant relationship" or "instant trust." These must be established over time, with consistent behavior. As a psychotherapist and through experience, I know that this is true. All people are complicated and multi-layered. What you observe on a first meeting is never the whole story.

I give you the analogy of an iceberg. The tip of the iceberg can be seen above the water line and is the least dangerous part. Any wise sea captain knows that when he sees an iceberg, he must slow down and proceed with caution, as the tip is 10 percent of the iceberg, while 90 percent is hidden below the surface of the water. It is the hidden base of the iceberg which is most dangerous and which, if underestimated, can sink his ship.

So it is with people. On a first meeting, we always present our best side. Like the iceberg, we present only the "tip" of our personality. We want people to like us. We consciously and unconsciously hide from people the deeper portion of our personality: our secrets, our failures, our shortcomings, the parts of ourselves that even we do not know. Most of us are capable of holding it together, presenting our best sides for a good length of time (weeks or even months). After six months of constant exposure in various situations, however, the hidden aspects of our personality will begin to emerge. The "real" person will begin to surface.

I encourage you in the Dating Phase of your relationship to take your time and get to know each other slowly. Enjoy this phase. Have fun. Plan social activities, do a lot of talking, meet each other's friends, get to know each other's interests, habits, culture, values, goals, family backgrounds and so forth. I would postpone having sex. Become friends first. Learn to know and trust each other. This is a wonderful period of discovery, and it can be enhanced by making each other feel safe, physically and psychologically.

I also encourage you to maintain your regular life. Go to work, see your own friends, do your exercise routine, have your own activities. Don't get too wrapped up with this new person in your life. I think women are guiltier of this than men. Women often neglect their women friendships when they meet a man they care about. They tend to lose themselves in a new relationship, catering to the needs, wants and interests of the man and neglecting their own interests and the other people in their lives.

Women often become too dependent on the man in their lives and then wonder what happened to their self-esteem. Men often complain that women become too clingy or stop growing once they are in a relationship. The very qualities that initially attracted the man to the woman erode away over time. Remember, in this phase you are responsible for your own body, mind, emotions and spirit. If you take care of each of your parts, you will remain vital and attractive to the other person.

While you are having fun in this phase, you should also be gathering information about this person of your dreams. What are you learning about this person over time? Are there parts you are seeing that trouble you or appear as red flags of warning? Please pay attention to these parts before completely giving your heart away. Refer back to your PARTNER "WISH LIST." Does this person meet your essential requirements? If you are not sure, I would, again, postpone having sex. Take time to gather more information. Be a careful listener. Does this person want to be in an exclusive relationship with you?

Keep in mind that once you become sexually involved, you will be much less objective. Does this person match the profile of your previous relationships? Refer back to your POSITIVE QUALITIES FROM PAST RELATIONSHIPS LIST. Take a long, slow look. This person may look different, have a different job but, below the surface, have the same personality traits as in your last relationship that did not work out.

What are you learning about their early and current life with their parents? What do you know about their past relationships and why they didn't work out? What are the characteristics of their living space and what does that say about the person? While you are at it, keep a careful watch over your own involvement in this relationship. Are you taking care of your body, mind, emotions and spirit? Is your needy Inner Child running the show? Are you able to postpone gratification? Are you using the logic of your cerebral cortex to gather data? Are you maintaining your own life?

MONETARY INVESTMENT

Another consideration in the Dating Phase is the expenditure of money. In the old days, it was common for the men to pay for everything. Today, however, most men expect that women will cover at least some of the expenses. And I think this is fair. You need to discuss it. Some couples begin by each paying 50-50. Others trade off, paying for every other date. Others, still, may have the man pay for outside activities, while the woman cooks dinner and entertains at home. Whatever you do, I think it is important to show appreciation. Sex should never be a requirement for money spent.

Sometimes, women who are codependent will rush in and pay for all the dates, as if they do not feel worthy of the man paying. I think this is a big mistake. In my experience, it is important for a man to make an investment in the relationship. Often, where a man's money goes, so goes his heart. A man who pays for nothing in a relationship is generally not invested in the relationship.

LEARN EACH OTHER'S GOALS

I also counsel women to let the man drive the relationship. What I mean by this is that the woman should let the man do most of the initial planning and let him set the pace of the relationship. My reasoning behind this is that men, more often than women, get frightened of commitment. If the woman is pushing him for too much, too soon, the man will frequently run away. If you let the man do the planning according to his comfort level, he won't get frightened and the relationship will proceed.

Of course, some men never want to proceed to commitment or marriage and the women involved with them eventually have to give an ultimatum. This is another reason to gather information early on: "What is your intention in dating me? Are you looking for a committed relationship? Do you want to get married?" Other times, it is the woman who does not want to move toward commitment and the man is forced to move on. At any rate, it is important to know your own goals and to ascertain if they are shared by the "person of your dreams" early in the relationship.

Chapter 17

COMMITMENT TO MONOGAMY PHASE

Eventually, any serious relationship will get to this phase. This is a very important phase in the life of a couple. The very act of becoming exclusive to one another establishes psychological safety and trust. It is an essential foundation for any long-term relationship. In essence, it establishes a boundary. It states that the sexual and emotional intimacy needs of each person will be fulfilled by these two people only. It declares that there will be no outside partners. It allows each person to give of their body, mind, emotions and spirit within a framework of safety and trust.

If monogamy is not established at some point in the relationship, each person will be left with feelings of uncertainty, fear and worry. Indeed, triangular relationships that involve more than two people seem to insure that no intimacy will be established.

Time, focus and attention will be split among many, guaranteeing superficiality, rather than depth.

Again, I do not believe sexual intimacy should take place until the commitment of monogamy is in place. There is too much for each person to lose. There is a higher risk of contracting a sexually transmitted disease. There is a risk of incurring a broken heart. There is a risk that your life's goals are at cross purposes with the other person's.

Men must understand that, for most women, having sex results in emotional bonding and a desire for commitment. This might have to do with the construction of the female body. Women's sexual organs are mostly internal and are designed to produce children. Women know there is always the possibility of a pregnancy, even if they use birth control.

In order to be ready for intercourse, most women require foreplay. They require kissing, touching and stimulation of the breasts and clitoris, in order for the vaginal liquids to be released to facilitate intercourse. Because the woman requires time and attention to arrive at an orgasm, she becomes dependent on her partner. When the woman gives her body, she is generally giving her mind, emotions and spirit as well. This partially explains why women don't usually want to have sex when they are angry, because their bodies do not respond when their mind, emotions and spirit are upset. Many women are not capable of having casual sex, even if they agree to it to please the man.

Many men, on the other hand, enjoy sex from a strictly physical point of view. They are attracted and aroused by what the woman looks like and how she dresses. Their sexual organs

178

are external and don't require a lot of stimulation. If the woman increases their arousal with deep kissing and petting, the man will want to release the built up tension. Men are tactile and visual. They enjoy touching the woman, entering her body, smelling and tasting her. They are often comfortable just having the sexual experience. Often, they often do not want any commitment and want to keep having physical experiences with many women. However, sometimes there are role reversals, where the man is emotionally bonded because he has sex, but the woman just wants to experience sex casually. If both parties only want to have casual sex, I would say they are not interested in a deep relationship and are only connecting with their bodies, not their minds, emotions and spirits.

Once you have both agreed to a monogamous relationship, I think it is important for each person to be tested for sexually transmitted diseases and to decide about the appropriate form of birth control. This requires adult level functioning and working as partners. Many times there is fear of being tested and a tendency to avoid it. It can be a bonding experience for you to go to testing together. Once you know that neither has a communicable disease, there will be a sense of relief and safety.

Often this very act will prompt you to disclose that you have some disease, like Herpes, which you have been too shy or embarrassed to tell your partner. You need to make a full disclosure. There is nothing like the freedom that comes from sharing some deep, dark secret. And in the telling, you get to see how your partner will react. Can he or she handle it? Does he or she shame you or reject you? Either you will establish safety, trust and acceptance or you will not. It's important to know at this stage of your relationship.

Birth control is the next thing which should be addressed. I have seen far too many couples who use abortion as a method of birth control. Abortion may seem quick and easy but, on some level, those who do it will pay a price. Generally, the price is paid on a spiritual or emotional level. It does not generate a sense of well being for a couple and should be avoided. It causes guilt, shame, doubt, distrust, anger, sadness and blame, which can haunt the couple for years to come. It often causes couples to break up.

Discuss which form of birth control is right for you. Today there are many options. I do believe that birth control should be shared by both people in the relationship. It should not be the sole responsibility of the woman. The man should consider wearing a condom or sharing the cost of birth control pills, a diaphragm, a spermicide or some other method. It's not about the money; it's about sharing the responsibility.

Chapter 18

ENCHANTMENT PHASE

In the beginning of the monogamous relationship each person is excited and happy. Each has found their true love and each feels safe within the relationship. Once again, I suggest that you really enjoy this phase. It is a time to delight in your love and mutual exploration. Both of you will be looking at the world through rose colored lenses. It will be as if you are both high on chocolate. You will enjoy every detail of your true love's body. You will find him or her amusing, stimulating and endearing. You will experience an increase in your energy level and your frustration tolerance. Your euphoria will spill over into every area of your life. You will delight in introducing your mate and telling antidotes about the relationship. You will want to spend most of your free time together. You will be amused and intrigued by the ways in which he or she is different from you. You will minimize any shortcomings and avoid confrontation. You will want this state of bliss to continue indefinitely.

From a psychological point of view, what is happening is that both of you are projecting your inner picture of the ideal mate onto the "screen" of the other person. It's as if we write a play or a movie that we want lived out. Your mate, being aware of the "script" and "role" you are writing, will try to live up to your expectations. They will try to be as perfect as you want them to be. You, likewise, will be responding to the "script" and "role" they are giving you. Both of you will try to be just what the other wants.

You want to believe your love is perfect and flawless; because of your love, you need this to be true. In addition, this person is giving you the opportunity to release your pent-up love, affection and longing. This person is giving you a chance to have your five basic needs from childhood met in present time:

- Love
- Safety
- Approval
- Guidance
- Respectful Boundaries and Consequences

Your Inner Child is delighted with all this. He or she feels that the new mate is perfect in every way, just like he or she wanted to have a perfect mother and father. So, in this phase, there is an "idealization" of the mate. As I said before, enjoy this phase and the lovely experiences it brings to your life. You will experience joy, enthusiasm, bonding, laughter, companionship, optimism; many of the qualities of being a child. This is a fun, wonderful period in the life of a couple.

Chapter 19

DISILLUSIONMENT PHASE

Unfortunately, the joy of Enchantment is eventually replaced by Disillusionment. This phase can be very painful, disappointing and sometimes fatal for a relationship. There is no exact time at which it occurs, but I would say that by the sixth month of the relationship, some disillusionment will occur. For some couples, it does not surface until much later. For these couples, problem areas and issues that were noticed in the early phases of their relationship were "swept under the carpet" and remained there for months and even years. This denial was like the proverbial "elephant in the living room." Everyone saw the elephant, but no one talked about it. Instead, everyone walked around it.

How do I define Disillusionment? I would say it is the disappointment that occurs when the "bubble of idealism" bursts, and you finally see the real person, with all his or her flaws and differences from you. In this phase, you begin to see the world through brown colored lenses. The mate is no longer perfect. In fact, you begin to see their flaws, short-comings and differences from you and you might feel angry and agitated.

To the Inner Child, this phase is devastating. The child needed and wanted the mate to be perfect. The child ran and hid his head in the sand at any hint of imperfection. Alas, it is the adult in you who eventually sees the whole person, through the lenses of reality. And, usually, you do not like what you are now seeing.

At this phase, you find things that irritate you. The cute little laugh now seems annoying. The nonchalant manner, in which they keep their house, now seems messy. Their clothing and hair cut choices become annoying. Their helpfulness now seems like controlling. Their willingness to go along with your wishes now seems spineless and indecisive. Their creativity which you originally enjoyed may be getting on your nerves. Their ability to manage their finances may now appear to be cheapness. Their availability to see you all the time may now feel like excessive neediness.

In short, the very differences which originally attracted and intrigued you, which seemed to help round out your personality, may now begin to repel you. My descriptions may sound funny, but, when these realizations happen, they are anything but funny. The confrontations that ensue are painful.

In this phase, you begin to confront the other's flaws or differences in a rather hostile manner. You try, once again, to "re-make" the mate into your ideal. But this time around, the mate does not oblige you. The mate sticks up for who he or she really is and says, "No. This is who I am!" "I am no longer doing things to please you. I am going to please myself. And, in fact, I think that I am right and you are wrong!"

This is a period of conflict, second guessing about whether you made a mistake in choosing this mate, anger, tension, sadness, turmoil and power struggles. Your own Inner Child might be throwing a temper tantrum. "I want what I want when I want it!" "I want this person to change!" "I want this person to be perfect!" "I want this person to go away!"

I would say that the amount of disillusionment is directly related to the amount of rose colored viewing you had going on in the previous phase of your relationship. If there was a healthy adult in charge, you probably saw the flaws and differences from the beginning and decided to love the person in spite of them. If your Inner Child was running the show, this will be a very painful, disheartening phase for you. Your disappointment in the mate will be matched by the disappointment you feel about your imperfect parents.

I encourage both of you to "hang in there." This, too, is a necessary phase in the life of a couple. It happens to all of us. None of us are perfect. None of us has it "all together." We all have areas in which we can improve and grow. The challenge here is: Don't think "It's my way or the highway." Explore your areas of conflict openly. Continue to make each other feel safe. Look at the good sides and the bad. Do they balance each other out? See if you can learn to tolerate and respect each other's differences. See if you can get over your disappointment and learn to love this whole, imperfect person. And give them a chance to love the whole, imperfect you. Many couples are able to survive this phase and move on to the next, deeper level of love. The love that develops is much more mature and realistic and tends to stand the test of time.

For some couples, the Disillusionment Phase might spell the end of the relationship. Take, for instance, when one of the people in the relationship changes from who they were in the beginning.

Let's say that in the beginning, your mate agreed with everything about you. Your opinions, your life style, your habits. Naturally, this person was easy to love. He or she loved you exactly as you were. Now, you are chagrined because this same person disagrees with you or finds fault with the essentials of who you are. "How could this be?" you say. "I am the same person now as I was in the beginning!"

What might have happened is that because of the love and approval they have experienced within your relationship, your mate has acquired the courage to disagree with you and may have evolved into a different *Self.* Your love enabled him or her to grow and change.

You, on the other hand, may not have changed over the course of the relationship. So, naturally, you fight the change in them. You want them to remain just as they were when you first met them, when they matched your "ideal" and didn't make any waves. You are alarmed that they might now want you to change. You might be unwilling or unable to change. Or, it might be that you are the one who has evolved and changed. You may now have different values, goals, interests or needs that your mate cannot or will not meet. Sometimes the changes in one person become incompatible with the other. When the changes are too severe, when they involve changes in the core of your being, the relationship does not usually survive.

DEEPER, MORE SERIOUS PROBLEMS

Another thing that can happen in the Disillusionment Phase is that deeper, serious problems emerge that were hidden in the beginning of the relationship. You find that you run into issues and dynamics that you never knew were there. Your ship, that is the "Relation Ship," runs into the base of the hidden iceberg. This person who seemed so perfect for the first six months begins to display some serious problems. You knew he liked to drink and have a good time, for instance, but now you realize that he is an alcoholic or drug abuser. He was able to curtail his alcohol or drug use while he was "under the influence" of the euphoria in the Enchantment Phase, but once the initial euphoria wore off, he needed his mood altering substances again. He might begin using them in secret, but, eventually does not hide the abuse and becomes verbally and physically abusive to you.

Or this person you thought was so quiet and easy going in the beginning of your relationship turns out to have a Major Depressive Disorder that has never been treated, which is now draining all the energy out of your relationship. You didn't notice it in the beginning because you were both high on the euphoria of the Enchantment Phase. But now you begin to notice that she and her home environment have a lot in common: There is clutter and disorder. Even basic daily functions are not being taken care of. There is a lack of energy and motivation to get things done. She no longer takes interest in you or your relationship. There is a dark cloud hanging over everything.

Or this person who was so sexually active in the beginning of your relationship is now totally disinterested in sex and turns you away. You learn now that the person you love was physically or sexually abused as a child and was so needy in the beginning of the relationship that they jumped into sex as a way of receiving love, affection and approval. Now that they feel safe, their wounded Inner Child has emerged. This child is too damaged to allow you to touch him or her. He or she recoils from even light affection or physical contact. You are not able to establish intimacy and are angry about being rejected.

Or the person you fell in love with because of her beautiful body turns out to have an underlying eating disorder. You find out now that she keeps her body thin because she is anorexic or bulimic. You find out that she never eats when she is not with you, or else she binges on food and then throws it up in the secrecy of the bathroom. You begin to realize that, although she is a beautiful, she has poor self-esteem, does not like herself and has difficulty establishing intimacy.

Or you find out that the mate who partially attracted you with his high profile job and substantial income has been hiding the fact that he cannot manage his money and has an extensive debt. You might find out that he is a compulsive shopper or gambler.

Or you may find out that your mate, who is divorced, has a chaotic, dysfunctional relationship with his or her former spouse or his or her children. As your relationship becomes more serious and demanding, the former spouse or children may become angrier with you and start acting out their anger or jealousy. These problems intensify if your mate does not maintain healthy boundaries to protect your relationship.

Or you find out over time that your mate has never emancipated himself or herself from their controlling, negative parents.

These are only a few examples. The list of serious problems goes on and on. The impact of a serious, untreated problem is enormous. It will affect your body, mind, emotions and spirit and those of your mate. If the person you love has a serious problem that is damaging your relationship, it is essential that they get help. If they are unwilling to do so, you will probably end the relationship. This is a sad reality for many people. The relationship seems to have so much potential and love, but the person is unwilling to go for help. There is a wounded Inner Child that is running their show. When you leave, they take their problem right into the next relationship, carefully concealing it below the surface of the water. Their wounded Inner Child is the base of the iceberg that keeps sinking Relation Ships.

Chapter 20

SURVIVING IMPERFECTION PHASE

I would say that the majority of my clients who are couples come to me at this phase in their relationship. Usually, they are on the brink of breaking up. They may be living together, engaged or even married. On the night of their first session, as they walk through my door, the tension is so thick that I could cut it with a knife. They sit on opposite ends of the couch. Their body language is closed and hostile. They do not look at each other, but stare directly ahead at me. I ask both of them why they are here and what they hope to accomplish in therapy. One or the other of them begins, "We have issues, problems. We are not communicating. We haven't had sex in a very long time. We talk but nothing gets resolved. I am coming here for help. I don't know what to do." Generally, the other partner says much the same thing.

As a therapist, my heart goes out to these couples. I see and feel their pain and anguish. It's an awful place to be. I have been there myself and know what they are feeling. To recall my experience, you can re-read the Introduction of my book. You will see that my husband and I went through all the Phases I have outlined. I tell my couples that they have already taken the first big step. They have admitted they have a problem they cannot solve by themselves, and they are asking for help. I reassure them that I can lead them through the process, if they are willing to show up and do the work. I have a very high success rate with my clients and many couples who seemed doomed to break up are now living very happy, healthy lives.

If you are one of these unhappy couples on the brink of breaking up, or if you become one of these couples, I suggest that you go to couple's therapy. If one or both of you has a serious problem, I would also recommend long-term individual therapy. I see many of my couples individually and jointly. Actually, I find the combination helpful because, seeing them together, I can better understand their individual problems and the reasons they are having problems as a couple. When only one person of the couple goes to individual therapy, he or she presents a biased report of the relationship. In the couple's therapy, the therapist gets to see the real dynamics and obstacles.

For couple's therapy, you should make a commitment to attend for at least three months. Don't look for a quick fix. Don't be impatient. Don't make any drastic decisions about the relationship. Don't expect the therapist to hand you a magic pill or to do the work for you. You and your mate must both attend therapy and do the work together. Generally, there will be reading and homework assignments to do between sessions. In my work with couples, I assign both people to complete my various Questionnaires in private and then we read and discuss their answers in our sessions.

1. Personal Inventory

2. Analysis of Childhood and Adolescence

3. Review of Significant Past Relationships

4. Partner "Wish List"

The Questionnaires generally provoke a great deal of discussion, often very heated. I use the discussions as an opportunity to teach my couples psychological and spiritual principles. I may also require them to read *"Facing Codependence: What It Is, Where It Comes From, How It Sabotages Our Lives"* by Pia Mellody and to highlight the points which jump out at them individually. We discuss their notes and feelings in our sessions.

I advise you to make a commitment to learn as much as you can about yourself, your family of origin, your wounded Inner Child and learn the same thing about your mate. Continue to provide yourself and your mate with safety and consideration. This is also the perfect time to ask for some Divine Intervention. We, as human beings, are fragile and short-sighted. When we ask for spiritual assistance, we draw from the power of the Universe and are guided to see the Big Picture.

Some couples come to me specifically for marriage preparation. They have not hit the Disillusionment Phase. They are deeply in love and are excited about their impending marriage. I ask these couples to commit to at least eight therapy sessions. I tell them that I have carefully planned these sessions to bring to the surface any potential problems they will encounter further down the road. I give them questionnaires to work on that facilitate this process.

Inevitably, the sparks will fly and some Disillusionment will set in. I tell them this is good. We want to expose hidden issues and damage from family of origin before the marriage. We want to learn about the Inner Child and the early coping mechanisms. We want to see what is buried in the unconscious. We want to hear the host of "family voices" and "family scripts" that are living inside them, prior to the marriage. We want to see the patterns they inherited from their own parents. We want to learn healthier, adult coping mechanisms and relationship skills. We want to do all the hard work prior to the marriage, so there are no surprises after the marriage. We want to prevent divorce and heartache.

In order for the deeper, more mature level of love to grow, all couples must be willing to work hard in this phase of their relationship. Love that stands the test of time is not automatic or magical. It is requires WORK, WORK, WORK.

In the next chapter, I am going to present some illustrations of the work my clients have done in therapy. I think that seeing how they have worked on their Inner Children will give you insight and courage to do your own work. I am deeply grateful to them for sharing their precious Inner Children and their vulnerability.

SECTION FIVE

A Collection of Inner Child Work

"Finding and healing the Inner Child
is the pathway to transformation."
~ J.D.

Chapter 21

DISPELLING STEREOTYPES ABOUT THERAPY

I want to begin this chapter by dispelling some stereotypes about therapy:

"Therapy is for crazy or weak people."

"Therapy is for women only."

In my experience with a wide variety of clients over a thirty-three-year period, the people who come to therapy are those who are strong and courageous. Generally, they are sensitive and intelligent and are searching for the higher meaning to life. They are not content to merely "exist." They are the ones who were different than most of the members of their dysfunctional family of origin.

They were not able to block out or deny the dysfunction. The dysfunction penetrated their bodies, minds, emotions and spirit. They, unlike the majority of people in our society, are not the "walking wounded," who walk blindly day after day, disconnected from their bodies, minds, emotions and spirit. The spirits of the people who come to therapy demand that they find answers to the deeper yearnings and questions of their soul.

These are the gifted members of our society. I like to call them the people who are "out of the bell curve." The bell curve is used in statistics to show where the majority falls. Generally, the largest proportion of the population falls within the bell curve. This is the common majority. People outside the bell curve are smaller in number than the general population and possess unusual characteristics which are not shared by the majority.

I have also found that many men do profound work in therapy, often on a deeper level than many women. It's true that many men do not initiate therapy on their own. Often they come in at the insistence of the women in their lives. Once they enter therapy, however, many choose to do their own, individual work. And their work is amazing! It's as if therapy finally gives them permission to be a "whole" person.

In the larger society, men are told that they are only important in terms of what they produce. No one really cares about their emotions and their spirits. Their bodies and minds are supposed to be strong and stoic, invincible to pain and pressure. They are competing in a world dominated by other men. There are constant territorial disputes, needs to "position one's self" and battles of "one-ups-man-ship." Men are supposed to amass power and money and prestige, at any cost. Men who do not are perceived as "less than."

Men, on the average, die ten years earlier than their wives because of these pressures. Their bodies produce heart attacks, strokes, cancers because of the pressures and lack of acceptable emotional release. Is it any wonder, then, that they do profound work in therapy? Therapy becomes the safe place, the place where they can explore their emotions and spirits. Gifted men are thirsty to do this work.

One last observation is that most of the women who come to therapy have problems with their body image. In society and advertisements, women are told that they have to be thin, beautiful, young, voluptuous and preferably white. Women quickly learn that if they do not possess the "ideal body characteristics," they will be less desirable and will have less power in their environment. The cosmetics, plastic surgery, clothing, and body and hair care industries are a testament to the problems women have with their bodies and their body images.

The Inner-Child work I am going to share has been done by my clients. These clients come from various countries around the world and different parts of the United States. They are children, adolescents and adults. They are single, married, divorced. They are heterosexual and gay/lesbian. They speak different languages, have different religions. What they all have in common is that they want to heal their Inner Children and live happier, healthier lives and are willing to do the scary work in therapy. It is my great pleasure to share their work with you.

Chapter 22

INNER CHILD WORK

HEATHER

I wanted to include the work of one of my adolescent clients, to show you how early people can be affected by the rigors and challenges in life. Heather began therapy with me at the age of 15. She had written this poem on her own, just prior to meeting me. When you read it, notice that she was in touch with her body and emotions. She was aware of her pain. She came to therapy to learn more about herself, to find someone who would listen to the yearnings of her heart and guide her in her relationship with her *Self* and others. She used writing as a means to express her emotions and spirit.

Heather felt alone in her family because her parents' time and attention frequently went to her youngest sister, who has special needs. She also felt "different" from the other members of her family.

Deepest Depression

A rose without petals
That's how I feel
A body without skin
A heart without a pulse
A cat with no hair
How do I explain the way I feel?
I feel as though my heart is crying
No one understands the way I feel
My Grandmother has died and I feel alone
She was the only one who understood me
Now she is gone and I am alone
Alone, alone. That word frightens me
Amma was the one whom I could
Confide in. How am I to go on
I know it will be hard
But I shall try even though I'll fail in vain
Right now I need someone to talk to
To share my life story with
Someone who will understand how I feel
I'll wait for that person
My heart is crying !!

Two years into her therapy with me, Heather drew the following picture. I had given her the assignment to draw anything she wanted to draw that day. I was teaching her to use art therapy as another method of expressing her emotions. She chose to transform my drawing of "Tomboy Judy" (which was hanging on the wall) into a new, happier girl. I think this is how Heather was feeling about herself. She was becoming more comfortable with herself.

Heather developed a seizure disorder at age 16, which was very difficult to control. She suffered through trials of many medications and their side effects on her body, at the very time when peer relationships are so crucial to one's self-esteem. She experienced her most dreaded nightmare — having seizures in front of her classmates. She had to transfer to a smaller school that was better equipped to deal with her seizures. Her ability to be a high academic achiever was diminished by the seizures. She suffered many losses, yet remained optimistic and hard working.

I am sad to report that Heather died at age 18, from a grand mal epileptic seizure. Thank God her spirit led her to therapy with me and others. In her short life, she was able to establish closer relationships with her *Self*, her mother and father, complete her Gold Award in Girl Scouts (the equivalent of being an Eagle Scout in Boy Scouts) and forge some success in friendships and the educational system. At her memorial service, many testified that they were touched and inspired by her life. She was a remarkable girl, with many challenges. Her courage and example brought other members of her family into therapy. I was blessed to work with her. This poem and drawing are part of her legacy and are offered here to help others, which was her goal in life.

KATHERINE

Katherine is a 51-year-old woman, raised by emotionally abusive/ toxic Jewish parents, whose presenting problems in therapy were a Generalized Anxiety Disorder, a Dysthymic Disorder, and unresolved relationship issues with her negative, controlling mother. She is in her second marriage, has one daughter, and works as a homeopathic doctor. Although she maintains a high level of competence in her profession, she is "hamstrung" in her personal life. She has difficulty setting boundaries with people, her body is in a perpetual state of tension and dread, and she feels angry and guilty about her codependent relationship with her mother. She is often unable to experience the joy, creativity and enthusiasm of her Inner Child.

In the course of our therapy together, I encouraged Katherine to journal her feelings and her dreams, in an effort to see the contents of her unconscious and to understand and learn to love herself. Here are some samples from her journal:

Wednesday – "I feel so sad, and I realize that I almost always feel sad, nervous, upset in my guts. I fear that I have spent far too long living a lie with my mother. God forgive me for my bad temper and weakness in not breaking away earlier or demanding that she stop [abusing me]."

Thursday – "Realizing again why I eat more than I am hungry for — because of my inner tension at my solar plexus. So much internal struggle. I feel wounded, raw, cut out in this place. I create physical pain so that I — Katherine — am reminded of psychic pain. I teach my students about how our physical issues point the way to old trauma, abuse. As I open my solar plexus and feel its hollowness of heated energy and fullness of food, I ask this place in my body to speak. I offer, "What can I do to heal you? How can you be free?"

I hear a child/teenager wailing, alone in a dark prison, bars on the windows. She sees the light outside but can't get out. The room is covered with mud and sweat and feces. Her hair is matted, her clothes shredded. Shackles of lies are on her feet, keeping her from walking freely. She is mad (insane) with grief and fear.

I cry for her and myself. It has been such a long time without contact. My mother is the warden of this room. She keeps all visitors away, along with all light, and all freedom. The young girl waits for mommy to come in and hold her, clean her, feed her, love her, but mommy stays outside with her beauty and whips, her tongue like a razor. She can only think of herself, not her own child.

I walk past this monster and talk, hold, clean my child. We make contact and she cries and cries. The world is so scary to her that she doesn't want to leave the room. So we stay put and clean ourselves and the room. We wash the room and, when clean, my bedroom as a child is revealed. As she cleans up I can see that myself is deformed, my face keeps changing shape. I can't hold onto myself. So I hold that girl, that self. I hold her until she sleeps and then I leave. I put flowers in all the corners and puppies in a basket for company. She, I rest in a place of beauty now. An angel guards this room. The beast at the door is crying as well. She wants to leave this place. She turns into a snake and slithers away. She is also me, the part of myself that is like my mother but yet it is not me."

As a result of her therapy, Katherine realized her Inner Child would never be nurtured by her toxic mother and that, she herself, would have to parent her Inner Child. Over the course of several months, Katherine began to set limits and boundaries with the people in her life. She stopped seeing her abusive mother. She let go of abusive people she had considered her friends. She paid attention to her emotions and body by a fashion and color make-over, buying expensive jewelry, creating her own jewelry, limiting the number of clients she treated each week and raising her fees. She enrolled in a graduate program. She treated her body to hikes and exercise, massage and acupuncture and better nutrition. She developed a more intimate relationship with her *Self* and her husband and sought out friendships that were nurturing. She learned to take care of her Inner Child.

HEINRICH

Heinrich is a 37-year-old, twice-married man who is separated from his second wife. He was raised by German Catholic parents who immigrated to New York. He started therapy with me when he was 33 years old and having serious problems in his marriage. Clinically, he presented with a recurrent Major Depressive Disorder, suicidal thoughts, and alcohol abuse. He admitted he had a history of being in codependent relationships. He was attracted to "needy" women whose lives were in chaos. His role was to "take care" of them. Their chaos and dependence provided him with an excuse to avoid his own problems, which were many.

Although he was a tall, handsome, jovial, high income producing salesman, he was sitting on a "toxic waste dump" of inner problems. His father was a harsh, cold, demanding man who drank too much and demanded perfection and manliness. Heinrich was a sensitive, creative young boy who was shy. He did not please his demanding father. His poor self-esteem was enhanced by being bullied and beaten by the kids at school because of his German name and his height. His mother was well meaning, but she babied and over-protected him, which thwarted his self-confidence and socialization skills.

He had few friends, so he learned to cover up his vulnerable feelings and stuff them in his unconscious. It is no wonder that he was the "perfect candidate" for sexual abuse by the parish priest/family friend. Finally, Heinrich had someone who paid attention to him. Finally, he had a source of love and approval. He was molested by the priest for six years (ages 10 to 16), right under his parents' noses. And, of course, he had never told his parents. Into the unconscious went all the feelings of betrayal, guilt, self-loathing, anger, sadness, hurt and shame. So, he carefully constructed an "alter ego" for himself, to hide the wounded inner boy. He became fierce and daring. He became a clown. He entertained and amazed the crowd with his many gifts. He found women to take care of. He used alcohol and rage to anesthetize any vulnerable feelings that broke their way to the surface.

We worked together in individual therapy for three years and he attended a therapy group of mine for one year. The group was for people who take better care of others than they do of themselves. The focus in all the therapy was for Heinrich to learn to set boundaries with his addicted wife, stop abusing alcohol, and learn to love and care for himself. We started by putting his outer life in order and then moved slowly into his inner life, where the wounded little boy lived. Although he had told me about the molestation by the priest in our first session, he was not ready to deal with it until the third year of our therapy.

The art work and writing that follows were done over the course of his year in group therapy. At the beginning of each group, the members were asked to draw something about themselves and write about their feelings or write about some topic I gave them. For each group member, art therapy and journaling were the media for getting to know themselves and, eventually, became "self-care-tools." Through these media, they learned to identify their emotions, tap into their unconscious, learn about their Inner Children and release the tension in their bodies in a healthy way. I will start with some of Heinrich's first work and progress to the most recent. Notice the progression. He starts with his outer world and gradually moves to his inner world, as he gains self-knowledge and the courage to peel away the layers of his defenses. We kidded him in group for his use of "bullets," but, then, they reflected his work in the business world and were a cute part of his writing style.

HEINRICH #1

HEINRICH #2

- (I) am way, way defensive .... always feel attacked!
- Deceitful, hiding money from wife (because of her shopping addiction)
- Excited (about making lots of $), followed by emptiness (who to share it with?)
- Isolated
- Hopeful
- Trying hard to control the un-controllable

HEINRICH #3

"How to "pull" the trigger on ending my relationship. Part of me wants to make it work. My heart aches at the thought of not being with her, while my head knows it's been no bed of roses .... Boy is that a gross understatement! What's the right thing to do?"

HEINRICH #4

"I'm feeling very torn over what I know (intellectually) I have to do with my relationship and feel (in my heart) I should do. I've been vacillating for the past 2-3 weeks. Nothing has changed in my relationship... I'm still unhappy. She has done nothing to warrant any change in my attitude. I feel like, no, I know I am doing things to intentionally hasten the break up. They're indirect and sometimes underhanded. I don't know why I just can't break the dependency directly."

HEINRICH #5

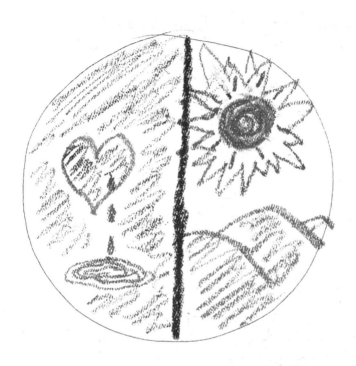

"How am I feeling about the upcoming holiday?"
- Unexcited – Ambivalence
- Dread – Hate that holiday is here. Kills 2-3 days of business in a very short quarter
- Lonely

"What things do I hate?"
- Hated my Dad's drinking
- Being away from friends and family

"How can I empower myself to have a good holiday?"
- Relax
- Sleep
- Don't over do it
- Surround myself with friends
- Keep busy

HEINRICH #6

BALANCE:
 EMOTIONAL
 PHYSICAL
 MENTAL
 PERSONAL

"Started talking about my molestation."

HEINRICH #7

"I am a confused, isolated, self-loathing child that yearned for acceptance, understanding, and self respect. I couldn't be heard, not by my parents, friends, or tormentors. The one person who listened (played off my pain) was the one person who betrayed me."

HEINRICH #8

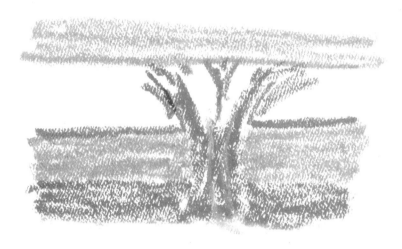

"The gray represents the moods, feelings, and troubles I've faced and am facing. An event happens to break me through one layer of shit, only to find another layer preventing a break-out. The green represents $$$."

HEINRICH #9

- I'm learning that it's OK to be scared, alone, angry — for the right reasons, myself
- It's OK to be happy, indulgent
- I'm learning to set boundaries
- I'm not always right, and that's OK
- I'm a survivor
- It's just as fun not to be smashed. Hangovers suck
- I can only control and correct those things I don't like about myself. I can't change those around me to make myself feel better
- I have GOT to expel the demons (my torturing myself over the molestation) from my being

HEINRICH #10

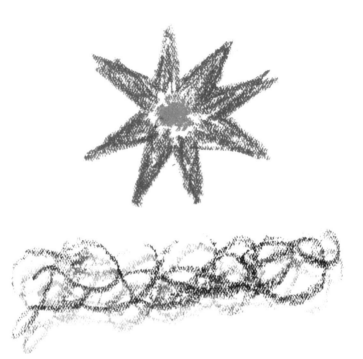

Peace

- Stability
- Fulfillment
- Backbone – Stand up for my wants and needs

Exorcize the "Demon"

- Spiritual connection
- Come clean
- Fight back
- Organize the chaos
- Make amends

HEINRICH #11

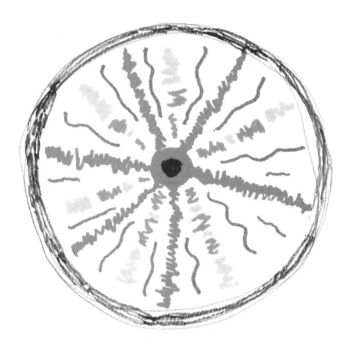

"My Former Self"

- Barriers to intimacy
- Anger
- Pain
- Fear
- Loathing
- Sheltered self
- Anxiety
- Depressed
- Suicidal
- No control

HEINRICH #12

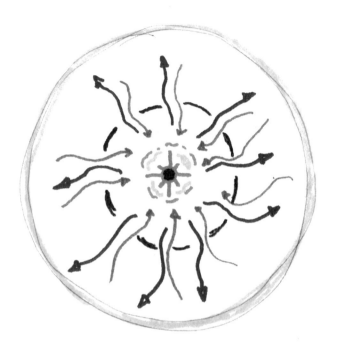

"My Newer Self"

- Happier
- Control
- Peace
- Openness
- Coping
- Acceptance
- Resilience
- Allow myself the luxury of feeling good

HEINRICH #13

"Goals for Group"

- Learn to focus on doing for myself and enjoying it without feeling guilty about it
- Continue to develop ways to manage and cope with stress
- Ways to accomplish this?
  Yoga........................NOT!!

(Note: Heinrich was receptive to most of my suggestions in Group. He did not, however, ever get into doing yoga)

At the conclusion of his year in the therapy Group, I handed Heinrich his folder and asked him to review the entire collection of his art work and writing. These are the observations he made about his Inner Child work:

"The first thing that comes to mind when I'm reviewing my previous drawings is the almost all too common split or layered nature of them. It reminded me of a split personality. I have this overwhelming feeling of being two separate and distinct people. The happy, gregarious person and the hateful, self-loathing one. The drawings are almost all orderly. But, in that order there is frequently chaos. It seems very emblematic of my life: orderly and neat on the outside, tumultuous on the inside. The one positive note in the drawings is that they have brightened up a lot. The tone is much more cheery then my earlier art work."

In the essays which follow, you will see some other insights Heinrich became aware of. Note how the experiences of his wounded Inner Child affected his life as an adult.

"Work is consuming such a large part of what I am doing. I literally work seven days a week. Not constantly, but everyday. It prevents me (does it really) from completing the simplest tasks? Work helps me withdraw from the crap in my personal life. It's one of the reasons I have such a shitty personal life. I have few interests (or passions) outside of work. I see others "living," while I'm existing! Physically, mentally, and spiritually drained. There are no other words to describe it."

"I am WAY too accommodating, at my own expense. I refer to it as being "wishy-washy"! I'm afraid to say "No" for fear of alienating friends and family. I need to gain a backbone, an ability to articulate my wants and needs in a clear and concise manner. My feelings, needs, and emotions can't take a backseat any longer. I want to accomplish this without appearing obstinate or belligerent."

Two years after graduating from therapy, Heinrich has gathered the courage to go public about his molestation. When he had talked to a district attorney three years ago, he was told that the case had exceeded the statute of limitation. With the recent nationwide expose of Catholic priests who have abused children, however, a newspaper journalist was interested in his story. Naturally, Heinrich now has to tell his family about his ordeal. Finally, his inner little boy will be vindicated. In addition, he is now happily remarried.

JACKIE

Jackie is a slim, attractive, blonde, 35-year-old nurse who has been divorced three times. She was referred to me by her psychiatrist, who is treating her for Bulimia, Social Anxiety Disorder, and Generalized Anxiety Disorder. She is taking the psychiatric medications: Celexa and Zyprexa.

In the beginning of my work with Jackie, the focus was on her marriage and trying to prevent another divorce. We had some couple's therapy sessions with her and her third husband. Over time, it became clear that she had married another "emotionally unavailable" man. The first husband was an abusive alcoholic. The second one was nicer, but was a workaholic. This third one has a Narcissistic Personality Disorder, which means, essentially, that he is in love with himself and has no love or empathy for her.

Bottom line, Jackie kept picking men who were guaranteed not to love her. Their rejection only made her feel worse about herself, which then reinforced her need to be thinner via Bulimia, in an attempt to be more beautiful and more pleasing to men.

The question was: Why does this beautiful woman have such poor self-esteem and what is she hiding inside? It took us two years in individual therapy to get down to her core issues. The closer we got to "the truth," the more frightened Jackie became. She became so frightened that she began missing scheduled sessions without canceling. I had to phone and write her numerous e-mails before I was able to pull her back into therapy. I told her that I suspected she had been relapsing with Bulimia and alcohol. I told her that the probable cause of the relapse was the progress she had been making in therapy.

She was living alone and learning to be comfortable with herself. She had begun eating more healthy foods, in moderation. She had stopped abusing alcohol and was exercising moderately. She had begun reading, attending junior college and developing her intellect. She confronted her belief that she was "dumb" and found that she was not. She had been setting limits with her current boyfriend, who seemed too needy. In short, Jackie had become a new person, a new version of herself. The problem, however, was that all this change frightened her. She was "outside her comfort zone."

When Jackie came back to therapy I was surprised to see that she had dyed her hair brown. "This is my natural color. I have been dying my hair blonde since I was 13. For some reason, I just decided to go brown again." My next surprise was when she said, "The reason I kept skipping my therapy sessions was fear of looking at my relationship with my mother. I have wanted to believe all these years that we have a good relationship, but I don't think it is true. I have been having terrible, recurrent nightmares the last couple of weeks. I have been abusing alcohol and medication again, and I have been having bulimic episodes, in order to escape these uncomfortable feelings."

The dreams that follow reveal the core issues that Jackie has been running from her whole life. Her core issues revolve around her negative, controlling, demeaning mother and her father who went along with the mother. Jackie's Inner Child is wounded. Her mother made her feel dumb and worthless. Her mother wanted to control every aspect of Jackie's life. At 13, Jackie stumbled onto Anorexia as a means of controlling her body and her life. Not even her mother could make her eat. She began bleaching her hair blonde.

Jackie's core issue is that she is "frozen in time as a wounded 13 year old," because her five basic needs were never met. As the oldest child, she put herself in the role of caretaker of her younger brothers. She tried to protect them from her mother's harshness and her father's indifference. She became the pseudo-adult, the false adult, who was really still a child.

Jackie struggled between trying to hold onto her individual identity and trying to gain her parents love and approval, which was an impossible task. In order to receive her mother's love, she would have to give in to her mother's controlling. So, Anorexia and Bulimia became her silent weapons in this family where emotions were never discussed. Later, she transferred her needs for love and approval to men. But she kept picking men who were unavailable, like her mother. Anorexia and Bulimia were methods of keeping her body childlike and pleasing to men. Blondes were supposed to be more desirable. Alcohol helped her cover her anxiety, pain and shyness. She became a nurse because she was a caretaker.

Dream #1

"My parents changed over the whole family. They couldn't taste food. They only drank blood. Everyone but me, I didn't want to change. I was slowly getting under their control. I could only taste a peach. I was throwing things, wanting to destroy their house.

"I was lying on the floor in my bedroom, holding on to my life, trying to keep it intact. They were taking things out of my room. I was lying on a blanket on the floor. They

226

yelled at me, "This is the way it's going to be!" It was my Mom doing the yelling. My Dad would follow behind."

Dream #2

"I was in a hotel, high up. All my three brothers were there. It was a really nice, high hotel. All of a sudden, there was an earthquake. "We have to get out," I yelled. We all started down the stairs and got scattered from each other. I tried one exit, to no avail. I got out another exit, got outside. I looked up and said, "Where is everyone?" I saw my brother. "Oh, my God, there he is!" I ran toward him. There were big arches above, that started to fall. We didn't get crushed, but ran back inside the hotel."

Other Dreams:

Recurrent themes of "yelling and screaming at my parents, wishing they were dead. Knives, hitting and scratching them, blood. Waking up and screaming at my parents."

Therapy has been the "earthquake" that is shaking up Jackie's house from childhood. She is finally ready to deal with her inner issues. Her spirit led her to dye her hair brown again, as it was when she was 13. She is ready now to explore her inner wounds and assume her authentic identity. She and her boyfriend are going to start couple's therapy, as both are willing to do the work to have a healthy relationship.

JOEL

Joel began therapy with me when he was at a cross-road in his life. He was in an eight-year marriage and had fallen in love with another woman. He felt guilty and confused. His indecision was compounded by the fact that he routinely smoked marijuana three to four times a week.

Joel met his wife when he was 19 and he was now 33. He was born in East Africa and lived there until he was 13. Joel inherited a medical condition from his father; Polydactyl, which means "many digits." Both his hands and his feet were deformed. He had four surgeries, when he was two, three, ten and eleven. He was usually in the hospital for three to four days and would have several months of recuperation and painful physical therapy after each surgery.

He grew up feeling self-conscious about his body and worked hard to hide his hands and feet. Interestingly, however, he worked as a professional drummer and percussionist. He had fallen in love with drums in Africa and could make wonderful music with them. But even in his work, he tried to fade into the background and be heard but not seen. Although he was a handsome young man, he had poor self-esteem and a certain level of shame about being physically different. He began using marijuana at 13 and it became a coping mechanism for him to avoid his uncomfortable feelings. He was a gifted writer, but he had trouble knowing or sharing his deeper feelings. He maintained a mellow, superficial image for the public and tended to be a people pleaser.

Our work together focused on him becoming abstinent from marijuana, journaling his feelings and dreams, and sorting out his feelings about his wife and the woman he had fallen in

228

love with. It was a very painful year and a half for him. For the first six months, he was separated from his wife, and then they mutually decided to divorce. Joel dealt with his profound sadness and the tremendous guilt about how his marriage had ended. His spirit was calling for him to move forward, but he did not know where it would lead him. He had depended on his wife throughout their marriage. Now, he was alone and afraid. He and his wife, supported by therapy and their personal strength, worked through their feelings and said "Goodbye" as deep friends. Each realized that something had been missing in their relationship and they were entering a new phase of personal growth. It was painful for everyone.

After the divorce, I worked with Joel to develop a relationship with himself and urged him to get to know the wounded little boy who lived in his unconscious. This was the little boy who had endured those painful, scary surgeries and had never really talked about it. This was the little boy who tried to hide his hands and feet. The writing that follows was an assignment I gave him: "Write a letter to your hands and feet."

To my dearest hands and feet —

I wanted to wish you the happiest of birthdays today. We've been together for 34 years now and I wanted to celebrate you most of all today….

I know I've written about my feelings for you before and I've thought about you in one way or another every day of my conscious life, but I feel like I've never given you a real voice in all of this; let you tell me how you have felt through all of our growing up together. Maybe we can find a little dialogue here today, on our birthday. I want to give each of you your own solo space and then I will return at the end. But before I let you speak, let me say how much I do love all of you, how much I want us all to be whole and at peace, and how very much you've meant to me all these years. Please do not be afraid to tell me anything and I will approach this with the same spirit.

LEFT HAND

I know I am the one who has caused you the most stress and discomfort, the one who is most visibly scarred, the one that attracts the most attention. I am sorry I could not have been born whole and beautiful and with all of my fingers functioning. I'm sure you've gotten used to looking at me by now, but I want to point out my features. I have a lovely thumb and index finger. They look like most anybody's, and they are pretty handsome if a bit stubby. I was a little sad you hurt my thumb playing football back in college and a little upset you never did anything to help it heal, and it set a little funny, but it did heal and it doesn't hurt any more.

My middle finger bears some scars. It used to be attached to my ring finger and still leans towards its separated twin. This finger has a Z scar on its inside from your 3rd surgery and that worked pretty well, helped it to bend. It doesn't straighten out, but it has a rather handsome shape to it all the same, especially the top half.

The ring finger is the elephant in the room, the one of us that stops traffic, that all of your fear and mistrust and shame points to. I know it's a strange one, with its Y bone and twin nails, and you've had to explain this one many a time, much to your discomfort. It has a scar around the middle from the plastic knuckle that never took. It can't bend and sticks out when I try to make a fist. It's scarred at the base too, where the knuckle meets the top of the hand.

I'm particularly sorry this finger made it so difficult for you to wear a wedding ring and that this did, in fact, hurt your marriage, that it opened the door to flirting and infidelity. Maybe you feel like you were denied some of the beautiful symbolism of being married. I know you have talked about wanting to have a special one made if you get married again and I would be proud and honored to wear a ring on this finger.

Then there's the pinky, a little knobby guy stuck on the end, not too unusual in and of itself, but a lot different from its counterpart on the other hand. This finger gets forgotten sometimes and it was never cut on, but it's a part of the hand, has all the same issues, and loves you just as much.

Together we do a lot for you. We hold a drumstick and, though we can't really form a traditional grip, we do very well with the matched grip and can even do an approximated half-traditional grip. And don't we do a great job for you on all the ghost notes and accents on the snare? Even your right hand can't do that as well as us! We hang in just fine for all the hand percussion, too. We can type and play piano and we've tried chording on guitar, too. We know we're not your dominant hand, but we feel like we hold up our end in all of the hand duties: Like a glove hand in baseball and support hand for the jump shot. We have a beautiful palm and we love to stroke and caress and make love, and we love to be touched.

It did hurt going through all the surgeries. We tried doing physical therapy for the knuckle that didn't take and maybe we gave up too soon. It was never any fun getting cut open. I know you can not remember the first two operations, but those were awful, they hurt, and we know you didn't understand. But it's not our fault. It's just us, the way we were put together, four & a half fingers and a thumb. All we've tried to do is love you and do everything you asked of us. Can you really imagine looking down at your left hand and seeing anything else than what you see? Isn't there something kind of cool knowing that there is surely not another left hand quite like us anywhere in the world?

Just love us and forgive us. We forgive you for all the times you were embarrassed by us or put us in your pockets or hid us behind your back. We'll always be together and we have to love each other. Don't be afraid to adorn us; we would love that.

RIGHT HAND

Not only do I get to talk about myself, but I have to do all the work for the others, moving this nice silver pen across the page! This is something I do for you every day; act as your instrument, your interpreter, the one who gives permanence to your thoughts and desires and dreams. So it's nothing new to be doing the extra work, but maybe you will remember how hard I do work for you and give us a little extra love for that.

We're not as immediately obviously unusual a collection of digits as our left brother, but we're unique all the same. Again, a fine, healthy, uncut thumb and forefinger, nearly identical to the left pair, grateful we have those to offer you and grant you dexterity. The middle finger is an odd one, though. The Z scar that didn't quite bring the finger all the way down and the extra little pocket of flesh that used to hold that pesky extra bit of nail — glad to have had that removed — and just a lopsided slant to the whole finger. But it's strong and fairly flexible. The ring finger still longs to be twinned to the middle; it leans over toward it like a flower seeking sun, and it's very thin and not too strong. But it does a great job of forming your unique "snap." It acts as a resonating board and launch pad for your thumb and this is one of its great shining achievements.

Your pinky is a funny one, all bulbous and so different from the left. It wears a ring well, probably the most natural of any of your fingers for wearing a ring.

All put together, we form a pretty functional hand. We do a lot for you besides writing. We do a great job for you drumming and we work really hard to help you earn a living. We play piano and love chording and helping you compose. We play percussion. We love playing sports with you and are grateful you have kept us free from injury.

Yeah, we're your masturbating hand, too, and you know we've given you a lot of good feeling over the years.

"We know we're the more subtle of the two hands; that if there were two like us, we might not be noticed together. But we've hurt just as much and been cut open just as often. Like our left hand said, we try just as hard to do everything you ask of us and appreciate that you don't shy away from putting us out there. We try to make the peace sign and the OK sign and even to flip people off if that's what you want our fingers to form. And we know we may not do those things artfully or gracefully, but we make the gestures anyway. We communicate for you and we carve the air when you speak and we are there for you. Don't ever feel like you have to hide us. It's been a long time since we were cut open and we forgive and feel content with who we are. We are yours. We'll keep writing and we'll work for you always. Please love us.

LEFT AND RIGHT FEET

We'll speak together to give the right hand a break! Thanks for the hard work, brother. We know we look pretty normal these days and we're grateful not to have to make you have to explain us away, but we all know we went through a lot of hard times together. That last operation for us was probably the worst you had to go through and we are sorry for that; sorry at how awful it felt and that you were laid up in a wheelchair all summer. We hated it. Hated having our little toes broken and separated and hated the raw new skin in between the toes. How much it hurt when Mom put the gauze in between the spaces, even though we loved her for doing it, and loved soaking them afterwards. We knew it was for the best. It made it a lot easier to wear shoes and it was a drag all those years when we were so wide that wearing shoes hurt and we would limp when we were running around wearing cleats and playing sports. We work so hard for you too. Not just the footwork on the drum set, or the balance we give to your hiking and climbing, but all the daily effort it takes to carry you around. We do it because we love you. Love us, too. Take care of us. Buy us beautiful shoes and keep our socks clean and free of holes, and we will always hold you up.

IT"S ME AGAIN NOW — ME AND ALL OF US

Oh, my hands and feet. How I have hurt and been afraid to show it. How I have wondered what it would be like to have normal appendages, how that would have changed my life, if I would be remotely close to the person I am today.

During all our operations I was so concerned with being a good patient, I didn't ever really let myself go; let myself show how much I was hurt. Whenever I did, it was forced out of me against my will and it was hard to breathe through and I hated it. I hated being in the hospital, eating the food, throwing up, going to the bathroom in the bed pan. I hated the stick of the I.V. needle, the shots, and being wheeled down the hall to the Operating Room. The horrible sick feeling, waking up in the Recovery Room after being 'out' for ten hours. The sense of helplessness and inevitability that accompanied my pain. I hated when Mom & Pops had to leave me at night. I didn't like having to put them through being with me and seeing me in so much pain. I wanted to be strong for them and I know it had to hurt to see their child hurting. Mom must have suffered so much and she had to be so brave and was something she chose, marrying into our hands, making this her life. And I've worried about how this would impact women in my life. Maybe this is a part of my sexual malaise; that fear of procreating, of making an innocent party have to bear the anguish that we all share. I don't know how anyone could have done a much better job than Mom did.

And Pops? All this traces back to him. I wonder a lot how he felt about all this growing up, without a parent to model the experience after; how that must have shaped him? I've never felt angry at him for bringing me into this world with this particular handicap. At the same time, I've never really held him responsible, either, and of course he is. If I can acknowledge that and forgive it maybe that would help. Maybe talk to him about how he felt going through his operations maybe that would open some of this up. I always felt loved and supported by him, but I think I also inherited a certain stoicism from him about the whole process; a sense of just "soldiering through," that did help in some ways, but has, maybe, hurt in others. I think it would be good to try to talk to him about that when I feel ready.

So many of my issues have to deal with attractiveness and desirability and comfort in my body and confidence in my appearance and balance and style and these all have deep roots in my hands. My sensuality, my trust in myself to allow myself to feel

I've never liked feeling ashamed of my hands or feet, but what hurt the most was just having them suffer. That awful moment of taking the bandages off, seeing them all discolored. That sinking feeling in my stomach. How will they ever heal and look beautiful? I can write and talk about them and heal my emotions, but I must make sure to make them feel wonderful physically now. Touch them, give them massages, baby them, adorn them, make them loved and beautiful.

"We've been together for 34 years and we will be together forever. Forgive me for ever being ashamed of any of you. We are all growing up and trying to learn. Let us all be grateful we are doing this now, while we are still young and in our prime and have so much to look forward to.

Love,

Joel

SECTION SIX

Working Together to Achieve a Healthy Marriage

*"True love: it isn't like the movies,
it's something for grown-ups"*
~ J.D.

Chapter 23

GENERAL COUPLE'S QUESTIONNAIRE

In this chapter we begin a dramatic departure from the first five sections of the book. The emphasis in the first section was on the individual. We looked at your family of origin, your developmental process, your coping mechanisms, your Inner Child, your desire to find "true love" and your courtship.

In this 23rd chapter, we shift our focus to the emerging "you the couple." The emphasis here is on two people, who will prepare for marriage and begin their lives as a married couple. The "two" will become a new entity.

I had a very interesting glimpse of this new entity this past weekend. My husband and I had gone to watch a Native American Pow Wow. A Pow Wow is a special event for Native Americans of various tribes, to come together and participate in dance competitions, drumming, singing and socializing. It is an opportunity for them to keep their native traditions and culture alive. The participants are old and young, men and women, teens and children.

During the dance competition, my eyes were drawn to one particular little girl. In the midst of the large crowd on the field, she seemed to be in her own little world. She danced with joyful abandon and had an endless supply of energy. Round and round the circle she went, never tiring and following her own inner leading.

I was so taken by this little girl that I felt compelled to seek her out. I found her in a tent, sitting with her grandparents, her parents and her brother. I told her parents she was my favorite dancer, and then, I gave the little girl the same message. She grabbed my fingers through the tent and indicated for me to meet her in front of the tent. I knelt down beside her and asked her how old she was. She told me she was only four-years-old and had been dancing for three years. We talked for some time, and then she said to me, "I want to meet 'The Other You'." At first I didn't understand what she meant. She had seen me standing outside the tent with my husband. In her eyes, he was "The Other You." We were not two separate people. We were two parts of me. It was a profound concept.

Marriage is the ultimate commitment. Two people vow to become "One." The limitations and frailties of the "two separates" are forged into a "One" that is stronger than the separate parts. It is a holy alliance which gives us the opportunity, through the intimacy and commitment, to grow into our highest selves. The friction of our differences rubbing against each other smooth and polish us. Our love and hard work together transform us from rough rocks into precious gems. Sounds wonderful, doesn't it?

I wish I could tell you that marriage will always be romance and star light, like a movie. The reality, however, is that, in many ways, it is harder to be married than it is to be single. When you are single, you can be selfish and self-centered. You can do what you want, when you want it. There may be loneliness at times and a desire to be married, but you are in control of things when you are single.

When two people become engaged and start the process of transforming themselves into a married couple, life becomes much more complicated. Instead of one opinion, there are two. Instead of one person making the decisions, there are two people vying for that role. Instead of one vision, there are two. An engagement is both an exciting and serious phase in the life of a couple. It is a time to plan "the ultimate party" and honeymoon. But there are ice bergs below the surface of the water which can sink this newly formed "Relation Ship."

The Questionnaire which follows has been carefully designed to expose the ice bergs, the issues which might threaten your lives as a married couple. This is an important questionnaire. I originally designed it for a beautiful young couple who were recently engaged and who had contracted with me for eight pre-marital counseling sessions. Since that time, it has been used by many engaged couples, couples who are living together and contemplating engagement, and married couples who have come to me for couple's therapy.

Whichever category you fit into, I think you will find this Questionnaire quite thought provoking. I suggest that each partner complete it in privacy, and then the two of you sit down together and share your answers, one question at a time. That is the method I used in my sessions. Take time to listen to each other's answers and dialogue about any issues that are raised. In my sessions, we often spent an entire hour listening to and talking about the answers to just one question.

SAMPLE OF GENERAL COUPLE'S QUESTIONNAIRE

1. Why do/did you want to get married?

2. Why do/did you want _____ to be your wife/husband?

3. What are the qualities and characteristics which attracted you to_____?

4. How do you define "marriage"? i.e. one equal partnership/entity; two equal entities; one head of household, etc.

5. Who will be/is in charge of the following, in the marriage?

- Earning the family Income

- Checking/savings accounts

- Monthly bills

- Personal expenses

- Big ticket item purchases

- Sex

- Household furnishings and decorations

- Chores around the house, e.g.:

  - Groceries

  - Food preparation

  - Laundry

  - Bathroom

- Kitchen

- Bedroom

- Vacuum

- Trash

- Ironing

- Child care

- Outside friendships

- Entertainment

- Deciding individual absences from the home

6.   How is _____ different from you?

7.   Who will decide where you will be living during the marriage?

8. How much personal time and space do you need?

9. How much sleep/exercise you do need?

10. Describe your eating habits.

11. Describe your spending, credit card, and savings habits. How have you handled debt?

12. What are your hobbies/special interests?

13. Who will/would decide if the names will be changed after marriage?

14. Do/did you want/plan to have children? How many? When? Are you using some form of birth control?

15. If you and/or your mate already have children from a prior marriage, answer the following:

     Describe your relationship with your own children:

     Describe your relationship with your potential step-children:

Describe your relationship with your ex-spouse:

Describe your mate's relationship with his/her ex-spouse:

Describe your relationship with your mate's ex-spouse:

Describe how your children feel about your mate, the other children, and your impending marriage:

16. Regarding your mate, which do you think is more important to him/her: The marriage/family? Or the career?

17. Are you neat and orderly, cluttered, or somewhere in the middle?

18. Who is going to plan and pay for the wedding?

19. Describe your relationship with your potential "in-laws":

20. Describe your mate's relationship with his/her own parents:

21. What is your spiritual belief system and is it compatible with your mate's?

22. Do you plan to practice a particular religion in your marriage?

23. Do you plan for your children to practice that same religion?

24. Are there any areas where you anticipate or experience problems in your marriage?

25. Describe your anger management and problem-solving style:

26. Describe your mate's anger management and problem-solving style:

27. In general, are you respectful of your own needs and boundaries and those of your mate? If not, explain how you are disrespectful of needs or violate boundaries (your own and your mate's.)

Do you make amends when you disrespect needs or violate boundaries? Are you able to ask for forgiveness?

Explain...

28. Describe your current sexual relationship:

29. Do you feel your partner is attentive to your sexual needs?

30. Are there any changes you would like to make?

31. Are you and your partner able to talk openly about sex and your sexual needs?

32. Are you currently indulging in food, alcohol or substance abuse or other addictive, mood altering behaviors (obsessive shopping, gambling, sex, etc.)? If so, are you in treatment or are you considering it?

33. What is your communication style?

34. What is the communication style of your mate?

35. What are your core values, goals and aspirations within the marriage?

36. What do you and your mate have in common?

37. Do you schedule special time together to keep your romance alive?

38. Do you and your mate agree on "parenting practices" for your children or your animal children?

39. Do you take responsibility to care for your body, mind, emotions and spirit?

Describe what methods you use.

40. If there are problems you cannot solve as a couple, will you be willing to work hard in couple's therapy to improve your marriage?

ANALYSIS OF YOUR CURRENT RELATIONSHIP

Once the two of you have shared your answers with each other, go back to your Questionnaires and circle the numbers of the questions where you are in disagreement.

1. List the numbers of those questions.

2. Re-reading those questions, which "issues" appear to be the most serious? Make a List.

3. In order of priority, work together to find a solution or a compromise. Then follow up the process with the other issues. If there are problems you cannot solve by yourselves, make a commitment to work together in couple's therapy and individual therapy.

Chapter 24

MARRIAGE OF TWO ADULTS AND TWO INNER CHILDREN

In this section, I want to reintroduce the concept of basic Emotional/Psychological Needs. In the first chapter of the book, I delineated the needs of the *child* in the family of origin. Here, I want to present the needs of *each partner* in the relationship/marriage.

When a couple marries, there is the creation of a new family unit. You come to the marriage as adults. It is important to recognize, however, that each of you brings your Inner Child and the influence of your family of origin. You are not just two adults coming together. You are two adults with two Inner Children. You may be aware of these Inner Children or they may be hidden in your unconscious.

Sooner or later, with the pressures, conflicts and challenges incumbent in establishing and maintaining a marriage, the personalities, wounds and coping mechanisms of these Inner Children will rise to the surface and affect the quality of your adult lives. When this happens, you will be confused and frustrated and may become over-whelmed. That is why it is so important to provide a protective environment for each member of the household. As trusted partners, you each have the unique opportunity to cherish, honor and provide a healthy environment for each other's Inner Child.

EMOTIONAL/PSYCHOLOGICAL NEEDS OF EACH PARTNER

1. Love

2. Approval

3. Safety

4. Guidance

5. Respectful Boundaries and Consequences

Upon reading these needs, you will notice that they are the very same needs as those of the child in the family of origin. I will explain each need now, from the point of view of the marriage.

1. **Love.** Each partner in the marriage needs to know that they are loved. Love cannot simply be a word that is used. It must be a daily action that can be felt and observed. You

must love your spouse and love their Inner Child. You must also love your *Self* and your own Inner Child.

2.   **Approval**. Each partner in the marriage needs to know that their unique identity is accepted.

3.   **Safety.** Each partner in the marriage needs to know that their body, mind, emotions and spirit are safe.

4.   **Guidance.** Each partner in the marriage has the obligation of mentoring the other partner in their growth and development, much like your parents were supposed to do in your family of origin. Only in the intimacy of a marriage will the personalities and wounds of the Inner Children come to the surface. Each partner may have trouble recognizing their own Inner Child. Therefore, it is the responsibility of each spouse to give feedback on what they observe. This feedback, this mentoring must be gentle and loving and motivated by the objective of healing and growth. This is a sacred trust — each spouse helping the other to become their highest, best *Self.*

5.   **Respectful Boundaries and Consequences.** Within the marriage, there must be rules of conduct that protect the integrity of each person. There must be an agreement about acceptable behavior and consequences for inappropriate behavior. There must be an on-going mechanism for evaluating the health of the marriage. Each spouse must feel safe to express their opinions, needs and concerns. When there is a boundary violation or disrespect of the needs of the other, there must be an apology and a sincere attempt to correct the behavior. Likewise, the person who has been offended needs to give forgiveness. Each spouse will find that they

fall short. We are human and we are frail. Each spouse must hold their own Inner Child accountable and must work toward *Self*-love and healing.

If you are blessed with children in the course of your marriage, these very same needs will exist for them. The needs of the children are as important as the needs of the parents. Likewise, any animal children you bring into your family have the same needs and require the same protection. If each member of your household feels safe, your family will thrive and each member will be blessed by interaction with the others. This is God's plan for you — to have abundance in every area of your life.

When I asked my husband to read this section which I wrote today, this was his response: "I like this part. It brings the book full circle. How about this as another way to help people relate to the concept of their Inner Child: when your spouse talks playfully, often in a child-like voice very unlike their normal speaking voice (like when you become little Judy), the Inner Child is revealing itself. I just happened to think of that when I read this piece."

Can't you see by his comments, how gentle and insightful my husband is? I am so proud of him! He is very strong and capable, yet also very gentle and wise. His feedback over the years has really helped me and challenged me to grow. I love his inner little boy. I would love to have protected him when he was a child. I can see in early photos how sweet and innocent he was. It is my honor to take the very best care I can of his precious little boy within our marriage. He, in turn, honors and protects and gives special attention to my Annie, Charlie and Judy.

With this talk of the Inner Child, don't be worried that I am saying you will only be little children in your marriage. Both my husband and I are strong, full functioning adults. We both run our own businesses, are very independent of one another and take our own responsibility to nurture our own body, mind, emotions and spirit. As adults, we both possess most of the qualities I mentioned in the section on Characteristics of the Spirit. We have formed a marriage based on love and mutual admiration for each other's abilities and strengths. We are both pretty complete in our development; balanced on both the right brain side (nurturing, loving, creative, spiritual) and the left brain side (organized, logical, able to put plans into action and achieve our goals.) We discuss our dreams and give each other insight about the message of the dreams. We discuss our un-conscious and the wounds of our Inner Children. After sixteen years of marriage, both the adult and the Inner Child parts of us feel safe and loved.

There is one other point I want to make about the needs of both partners in the relationship/marriage. Your marriage will also provide an opportunity for you to acquire the psychosocial developmental skills you did not master in your family of origin. To review those skills from the first chapter of the book, I will restate them here and explain how they can be acquired within the context of the marriage.

PSYCHOSOCIAL DEVELOPMENTAL SKILLS

1. Trust

2. Autonomy

3. Initiative

4. Industry

5. Identity

6. Intimacy

1. **Trust**. If the basic Psychological/Emotional needs are protected and provided for within the marriage, each partner will be able, through time, to learn to trust — themselves, the partner and greater society. If you come from a very dysfunctional family of origin, the learning of trust will take time, often years. In my own case, I would say it took me at least seven years to fully trust my husband. I had to see and experience on a day-to-day basis that he truly loved me, under all circumstances, and was not going to abandon me. I also had to see that he was a responsible, capable person who could shoulder responsibility and allow me to lean on him.

   When I finally learned to trust him, I saw a shift in my approach to other people. Rather than being aloof and contained in my own protective bubble, I began to open up with other people and share on a much more intimate level. Sometimes he jokes about how much I have changed. I can tell you that because I trust and feel safe within my marriage, I am a much more relaxed, fun-filled person.

2. **Autonomy**. If you came from a family of origin that shamed you or controlled you or didn't want you to grow up, you will enter your marriage with feelings of shame, self-doubt and timidity. Within the safety of your marriage, you will have the opportunity to grow, expand, learn new skills,

develop your abilities and become more autonomous. You will feel pride in your *Self*. It is an exciting experience.

3. **Initiative**. Within a marriage, there are countless opportunities to grow and expand. Rather than living in your parents' home or living with roommates or living as a single person, you will be faced with forging a home of your own with the person you love. You will learn to care for your home, care for your mate, care for your children and develop your own traditions. This, too, is an exciting opportunity. Having left your family of origin, you can decide who you want to be as an adult. You can learn new, healthier coping skills. You can learn to know and love your *Self*, as well as your mate.

4. **Industry**. Industry implies that you will learn cooperation and the ability to learn from others, to accomplish mutual goals. This can be quite a challenge in a new marriage. I will address the challenges in the section that follows. Industry is a skill that is hard to acquire when you are a single adult. Only a marriage can give you the full opportunity to acquire it, because in a marriage, you have made a commitment that you will not run away when the going gets tough. If you are merely living with someone, you know deep inside that you can escape or leave if you become too uncomfortable. You have not made a full commitment.

Scripture talks about the raw ore being placed in the blazing hot furnace, in order for the dross, the impurities, to melt away. Then, only the precious metal will remain. Marriage is that kind of furnace and crucible. The challenges and commitment will test us and mold us into becoming our highest *Selves*. Our defects will fall away and we will be transformed.

5. **Identity**. Within the safety of the marriage, you have the opportunity to become the full person God intended you to be. In your family of origin, you are often pressured to be who your parents want you to be. If your family was dysfunctional, your Inner Child would have been stifled in his or her growth. With a loving mate to encourage and support you, you can now grow into your full personhood. With the challenges of life in a marriage, you can develop your inner strength and find your true identity.

6. **Intimacy**. I would say that true emotional intimacy is the hardest skill to master. It requires that you must first have an intimate relationship with your *Self* — body, mind, emotions and spirit. It also requires that you feel safe and can trust your *Self* and the other person in the relationship. Once you experience trust and intimacy within your *Self*, you can transfer that skill to your relationship with your mate, your children and your other relationships. To achieve that skill, I suggest you return to Section One and review the suggestions found in Chapter 5 on "A Holistic Commitment to Your *Self*: Why it is your responsibility and how to do it."

Finally, in the Appendix, where I present the direct passages from Erik H. Erikson's *Childhood and Society,* you will notice that he identifies two additional psychosocial developmental skills that need to be acquired in one's lifetime.

7. **Generativity**

8. **Ego Integrity**

At your leisure, you can read what he has to say about these two additional skills. Generally, these skills are acquired in Middle Age and Old Age. Once again, there is a higher probability of acquiring these skills when you are in a healthy marriage.

To help you and your partner assess whether your relationship/marriage is healthy, I am going to give you the following assessment tool, which can be used throughout the course of your marriage. It is meant to be "organic," a living tool that will keep you appraised of the "health status" of your relationship.

ASSESSING THE HEALTH OF YOUR RELATIONSHIP/MARRIAGE

My Self

Adult

Inner

Child

My Spouse

Adult

Inner

Child

MY EMOTIONAL/PSYCHOLOGICAL NEEDS

On a scale of 1(least) to 10 (most), evaluate whether your FIVE EMOTIONAL/PSYCHOLOGICAL NEEDS are being met within your relationship/marriage.

LOVE

1· · · · · · · · · · · · · · 5 · · · · · · · · · · · · · 10

SAFETY

1· · · · · · · · · · · · · · 5 · · · · · · · · · · · · · 10

APPROVAL

1· · · · · · · · · · · · · · 5 · · · · · · · · · · · · · 10

GUIDANCE

1· · · · · · · · · · · · · · 5 · · · · · · · · · · · · · 10

RESPECTFUL BOUNDARIES AND CONSEQUENCES

1· · · · · · · · · · · · · · 5 · · · · · · · · · · · · · 10

MY PSYCHOSOCIAL DEVELOPMENT SKILLS

Write down this List and circle the skills you have mastered and employ within your relationship/marriage. Put a star by the skills you have not acquired or are not using.

1. Trust

2. Autonomy

3. Initiative

4. Industry

5. Identity

6. Intimacy

COPING MECHANISMS

Write down this List and circle the coping mechanisms you most frequently use within your relationship/marriage that help you deal with stress and problems. Put a star by the coping mechanisms you used in childhood.

Denial

Minimization

Repression

Fantasy

Avoidance

Displacement

Dissociation

Withdrawal

Addictions (alcohol, drugs, sex, gambling, shopping, etc.)

Disorders (Eating Disorder, Major Depressive Disorder, Anxiety Disorder, etc.)

High Achievement/Perfectionism

Loss of Memory

Reaction Formation

Obsessive/Compulsive Thinking or Behavior

Intellectualization

Rage

Busyness

Altruism (Service to others)

Humor

Idealization

Passive Aggression

Projection

Self-Assertion

Lying

Talking to others about my problems

Seeking professional help

Praying

Journaling

Using my support system

Reading self-help/inspirational books

Participating in a Twelve-Step Program

Yoga/meditation

Exercise

Gardening/Spending time in nature

Music or creative outlets

List any other coping mechanisms you use

You and your partner should complete this assessment independently and then discuss your answers with one another. Does your relationship/marriage appear to be healthy for both of you? If it is not healthy, are you willing to face the problems and work to improve it?

I will tell you that if your basic Emotional/Psychological needs *are being met,* you will have a healthy relationship/marriage and you will learn and use most of the Psychosocial Developmental Skills. In addition, because your *Adult* feels happy and secure, you will handle most of life's pressures with age appropriate, healthy coping mechanisms. Your Inner Child will also feel happy and safe and will infuse your life with energy, enthusiasm, joy and creativity.

On the other hand, if your basic Emotional/Psychological needs *are not being met*, you will have an unhealthy relationship/marriage — which will put your *Adult* and your Inner Child at great emotional and psychological risk. You will not learn or employ the Psychosocial Developmental Skills of trust, industry (cooperation) or intimacy. Rather, you will be autonomous of one another, each suffering your own misery. You will most likely cope with your pain, emptiness, sadness and anger by using the maladaptive coping mechanisms of your Inner Child. In this scenario, you will have re-created your dysfunctional family of origin.

Many of you will determine that your marriage is only partially healthy — some of your basic Emotional/Psychological needs are being met, and you have mastered and are using some of the Psychosocial Developmental Skills. In addition, you use a mixture of coping mechanisms, some of which are the maladaptive ones of the Inner Child and others are the healthier choices of the Adult.

I pray you will make the commitment to have a healthy relationship/marriage. It does not come naturally to most of us. We have to work hard to achieve it. I am telling you that IT IS POSSIBLE, and I believe it is what God has intended for you.

TRANSFORMATION OF MY *SELF*
INTEGRATION OF *ADULT*/INNER CHILDREN

With Transformation and Integration,
the *Adult* and Inner Children become one *Self:*
overlapping, accessible to one another

Chapter 25

THE ENGAGEMENT/WEDDING

I believe a formal engagement is a necessary "rite of passage" for a couple who are planning to get married. I think there are reasons why certain customs have survived.

The way I see it, an engagement is the couple's announcement to the world that they are going to get married. It gives all parties the time to prepare for change. The engagement serves as a transition between single life and married life. It is a time to plan and work together as a couple in the creation of the marriage. It is a time to emancipate from the families of origin and to develop one's own, married entity. This is an important working phase for the couple. It is a time to face the issues identified by the General Couple's Questionnaire and to resolve them. Resolutions of conflict achieved during this phase pave the way for a successful marriage and prevent volatile, unexplained eruptions after the wedding.

I think it is important for each partner to be actively involved in the engagement phase. Many times, the man makes the proposal and buys the engagement ring, then relegates the rest of the engagement and wedding planning to the future bride. Or it is the woman who rushes forward to micro-manage all the decisions and details, without considering the man's wishes or his need to be acknowledged.

In this section, I will identify some key elements of the engagement planning and make my recommendations.

The Proposal

Most often, it is the man who makes the proposal, but that is not always the case. The important part is that one person decides to marry the other and makes the request. From a woman's point of view, women want the proposal to be romantic. They want the man to take the time and effort to set it up romantically. I love to interview newly engaged couples and hear the details of the proposal and selection of the engagement ring. Men can be very sweet and creative and, when they are, they are sure to win the hearts of the women who love them.

The purchases of an engagement ring for the woman and an engagement gift for the man are significant. The expenditure of money, thought and effort on behalf of the other are symbolic. The price and characteristics of the ring and gift should fit what suits the couple. This is also the time to consider wedding bands, which are a societal symbol of the union. For some couples, however, these expenditures are not possible — due to financial struggles or the preference to save their money for the down payment on a house or a place to rent. The important element is that they work together to achieve their goals.

The Wedding Ceremony

A wedding and a reception provide an opportunity for the couple's families and friends to participate in the creation of the marriage. It is an exciting time for everyone because the entire world loves to see love. It is one of the happiest events in the life of an extended family.

Here again, the ceremony and reception should fit the personality, values, and desires of the couple. It is your wedding, regardless of who is paying for it. This raises the issue of the role of both sets of parents. Many parents believe that if they are paying for the wedding or reception or rehearsal dinner, they have the right to impose their wishes or demands.

I advise any couple who is working with me to establish boundaries with their parents. Remind them that it is your wedding and that you will make the final decisions. This is an important point. When you set boundaries with your parents, you are setting the stage and climate for your marriage. You may choose to incorporate some of your parents' values or customs or ideas, but it will be your choice and ultimate decision. You are establishing a separation between you and your parents and transferring your allegiance to your spouse. This is the foundation for a solid marriage.

Present day weddings have become very expensive. In many cases, they appear too extravagant. The excess money might be better served to help the couple make a down payment on a house or to set up their household. In some cases, the wedding and reception are more expensive than the couple can afford, which saddles them with debt.

I recommend that the engaged couple set up a realistic budget for the wedding, reception and honeymoon. If the parents are paying, I suggest you sit down with both sets of parents and discuss what is affordable. Don't push your parents to give more money than they can afford. If their money is limited, cut your budget or provide some of your own money.

For younger couples, it is customary for the Bride's family to pay for the wedding and reception and for the Groom's family to pay for the rehearsal dinner. Sometimes the Bride's family is not in a position to pay. Sometimes the Groom's family will step in to cover the short fall. Or vice versa. It is important to respect each set of parents. You don't want to start your marriage with ill feelings between the two sets of parents.

When couples are older or have been previously married, they often assume responsibility for all the expenses.

I think it is important for both the Bride and the Groom to plan the wedding. It gives you an opportunity to develop your "couple process." When you plan and discuss the details, you form a dialogue, create your vision and work together to solve the logistical problems. It's fine to delegate responsibility according to each other's skills and interests. It is not fair for one person to do all the work and it precludes your working together as a team.

Planning and pulling off a wedding is a lot of work! There are questions of:

- Budget
- Location
- Guest List
- Invitations
- Clergy or Officiator
- Vows
- Flowers
- Music
- Wedding attire
- Bridesmaids, Groomsmen, Maid of Honor, and Best Man
- Parents' roles
- Photographers
- Reception

I love to attend weddings where you see the personality of both the Bride and Groom reflected. It can be quite charming!

Some couples decide to dispense with the work and expense, and elope. This can be a good alternative. In these cases, however, I think it is a smart idea to have some sort of reception afterwards for family and friends. Generally, the people who love you want to share the excitement and participate in some part of the process.

It is normal for both partners to "get the jitters" shortly before the wedding. Occasionally, however, one person will get an inner warning or intuition that the wedding should not take place. I strongly urge you to discuss your feelings openly and then decide the best course of action. Although it is heart wrenching and extremely difficult with plans made, invitations sent, wedding gifts received and the hopes and dreams of the partners pinned on the wedding, it is better to postpone or cancel a wedding than to go through with it and end up in divorce. It is painful to cancel a wedding, but it is even more painful to get a divorce.

The Honeymoon

It's great when the newly married couple have the time and opportunity to unwind after the wedding. This, too, is a transition period. It is a time to relax, have fun and be alone together before you start your new life as a married couple. It's time to be romantic and childlike.

All too soon, the responsibilities of marriage will begin — where the adult functioning must take over and the Inner Children submerged. Speaking of children, the Honeymoon can result in a pregnancy you had not planned. Discuss birth control before the Honeymoon and take responsibility to prevent an unwanted pregnancy. Couples who get pregnant too soon can feel trapped and resentful.

The fun and enjoyment of the Honeymoon must be remembered and replicated throughout the marriage. It is important to keep the romance alive, especially when we get bogged down in the demands and responsibilities of our jobs, our obligations and our every day lives. If you are unable to have a Honeymoon after your wedding, don't despair. You can plan one some time in the future. It will provide you and your spouse the opportunity to fall in love again and bond, body, mind, emotions and spirit.

SECTION SEVEN

*D*EVELOPING
*R*ELATIONSHIP *S*KILLS

*"Becoming a healthy couple is a slow process that requires a
lot of work and the acquisition of specific skills."*
~ J.D.

Introduction to
Section Seven

I like to use the example of growing roses. Everyone loves a beautiful rose garden. It is fetching to the eye and delicious to the senses. The roses, in their various colors, call you to slow down, walk closer and take a long, slow sniff. On first inspection you only see the beauty of the flowers and the petals. If you reach out to touch them, however, you can be pricked by the vicious thorns on the stems. Nature armed roses with sharp thorns to protect their delicate petals from predators.

So it is with a beautiful relationship. It is wonderful to be in one, and other people are attracted when they see one. But like the rose, while there is beauty, there is also danger. There are thorns in every relationship which can deeply cut and wound the two partners.

I firmly believe that budding and long-term relationships require a great deal of attention and protection. Just as there is a positive Force in the universe that wants you to be happy and successful in your relationship, I believe there is also a negative Force that wants you to fail. The intention of the negative Force is to "divide the house," break up the couple, so that the awesome power of united love will not prevail.

In the following chapters, I am going to identify key areas that need attention within your relationship, and I will provide you with specific coping strategies and tools to empower your healthy, long lasting relationship and marriage.

DIFFERENCES: WHAT ORIGINALLY ATTRACTED YOU AND NOW REPELS YOU MUST BE UNDERSTOOD AND RESPECTED.

There will come a time in every relationship when the differences between the two people will become pronounced and aggravating. This is human nature. We all tend to be egocentric. Each partner will see the world through their own set of lenses and according to their own personality, characteristics, needs and wants. When the partner does not act or respond in the manner they want, there will be a tendency to judge, devalue or vilify the other. At this point, the couple can become embroiled in an angry power struggle. The smallest tasks or decisions can turn into nightmares of recurrent conflict.

I like to use the example of a simple thing like preparing a bowl of fruit. My husband and I would get into lengthy arguments about how to properly cut the fruit. He was convinced that his way of peeling and cutting an apple was best. His method was to take the apple in his hand and to make a series of rapid, small cuts of the skin with the peeler, shooting the small pieces of peel in every direction. He would then core the apple and make precise, geometrical slices of the apple, carefully trimming off any of the remaining core

I, on the other hand, was very proud of holding the apple in one hand and carefully peeling the skin off the apple in one continuous, graceful spiral, top to bottom, just as my Grandmother had done. Having done the artful part, I would core the apple and nonchalantly cut it into pieces. I didn't bother to remove any residuals of the core. I thought my method was beautiful and that his was messy. He thought that his method was the best and only way, and my way of peeling was too time consuming and my slices were imprecise.

The bottom line is that neither of us was "right" or "wrong." We were different. Each of us had our own particular styles, and both of us produced a bowl of fruit which we enjoyed eating! It took us several years to realize that we were "on the same team" and that we did not have to be adversarial about our differences. We learned to respect and trust each other and to embrace our differences. If one of us was more gifted or skilled in a particular area, we could defer to that person to solve the problem or meet the goal of the couple. There were no rigid roles assigned according to sex or societal expectation. We were free to be ourselves and to bring our uniqueness to the needs of the relationship. Each of us felt loved and valued and appreciated

COMPROMISE: A "FOUR LETTER WORD" THAT IS THE HEART OF PROBLEM SOLVING.

You may be wondering why I called compromise a "four letter word." For me, the vile swear words I use when I am angry generally have four letters: damn, shit, the "f" word, etc. Compromise, with its implication that I would not get my own way, seemed like a vile swear word to me. I hated the word! When my husband and I were engaged in power struggles, the last thing I wanted to do was compromise. I wanted to win! I wanted to be right! I wanted it my way!

It took me several years to learn that power struggles were exhausting and drained the fun, life and growth out of our marriage. Even if I won, the battle was so exhausting that there was no joy in the victory.

Compromise implies a coming together, a coming toward the center. Instead of being a dirty word, it conveys the essence of a marriage. **Two different people come together for the expressed purpose of love and a life together.** For that union to be successful, neither can remain exactly who they were when they were single. Both must be willing to be modified and reshaped into a better, higher *Self.* The very act of coming together implies that they will challenge, inspire, encourage and support the other to grow. Both partners must be up to the task and embrace the transformation from the single "I," to the collective "We."

When you as a couple are challenged to solve problems, look for a compromise. Draw from the ideas and skills of both partners to find a solution. This is a skill which will breathe life, satisfaction and mutual admiration into the relationship. *Embrace it!*

Chapter 26

BOUNDARIES:
Understanding the "What" and "How"

"Boundaries are essential for establishing individual identity, and maintaining trust between individuals."
~ J. D.

A "boundary" can be defined as: "The amount of physical or psychological space that you need between you and another person."

The quantity of space you need will be dependent upon your prior life experiences, your trust level with your *Self* and your trust level with other people. If you feel safe and happy with a person, you won't need much space between you. In fact, you might not want any space at all when you want to be intimate; you want them right next to your skin and psyche. On the other hand, if you are angry with someone or feel you do not know or trust another person, you will want a great deal of distance between the two of you.

People with different temperaments have varying needs for space. Introverts like to be quiet and alone. They are nurtured by lots of space. Extroverts are energized by many people sharing a common space.

A boundary can also be defined as the ability to say "No" to a request from another person. Each partner in a relationship has the basic right for their boundaries to be respected and honored. Boundaries make us feel safe and protected. They are like protective fences or doors and windows that can be opened or shut according to the needs of the people who live inside. If a person's boundaries are violated, there will be serious consequences. The person who is victimized by the intrusion will be angry, hurt, distrustful and resentful. If there is no trust, intimacy will not occur.

I believe that boundaries are the most important building block for the establishment of a relationship with our *Self* and other people. Indeed, boundaries are the foundation for any relationship. They keep people safe, emotionally and physically. Because this concept is so important, I am going to explore the concept of boundaries in greater detail.

I will begin by giving you some examples of healthy boundaries. The first one is an analogy with state and national borders. As you travel from one state to another or one country to another, you will experience crossing a border. There are physical signs posted which tell you which state or country you are entering. There are rules and regulations for crossing the border. For instance, when traveling by car and crossing the border from Arizona or Mexico into California, you must stop your vehicle at the border and answer certain questions posed by the border authority. For instance, "Where are you traveling from? Are you carrying any fruits and plants?" The border officer may ask to inspect your vehicle, your driver's license, your passport. If you are not in compliance with the laws of California, you may be detained by the border officer or required to leave suspicious fruits or plants. Each state and country has the right to post their borders and subject those who enter to inspection and regulation. People who want to enter have a choice whether to comply with the regulations or risk expulsion. The border signs are a visual, physical demarcation and the geographic borders encase a physical entity, with ideological components, rules and regulations and resources.

As individuals, each of us is like a state or country. We have a visual, physical presence and within our borders we have psychological, ideological, emotional and spiritual components. In an ideal world, each of us would be aware of our borders and our components and we would maintain healthy boundaries that protect us and allow us to maintain healthy, safe relationships with our *Self* and others.

Another example of a healthy boundary is: "I know who I am and what I need and want and I have the right to maintain my *Self.* I know what is Me, where I begin and end, and what is You. We are two separate people. I know how much space I need between you and me. I have rights and so do you."

Unfortunately, most of us do not understand the concept of boundaries. We are not taught about healthy boundaries in our homes or in our schools.

Our first experience with boundaries comes from our relationship with our parents. Few of us come from families that have healthy boundaries. Many of us were raised in families that had no boundaries, confusing boundaries, harsh boundaries or violations of boundaries. Subsequently, we did not establish basic trust with our parents or our *Self* and we were unable to establish a sense of our own identity. Because we do not have a stable, separate identity, we are unable to establish healthy boundaries. Because we do not feel safe or others do not feel safe around us, we are unsuccessful in our attempts to establish love and intimacy.

I will give you some examples of unhealthy boundaries:

- Inside their bodies, many people have rigid boundaries which cut off one part of their person from the other parts. This would be the person who lives in their head and is cut off from the neck down, unaware what is happening in their heart, body, emotions and spirit. They have rigid internal boundaries which prevent them from having a relationship with their *Self*. Because they are cut off from their *Self*, they may need food or drugs or alcohol to make them feel better or not feel at all. They will have difficulty establishing a relationship with another person because they do not have a relationship with their *Self*.

- Some people have no boundaries and are victimized by others. They are easily recognized by predators and others who would manipulate them for their own purposes. These people live in fear of being abused and, because they have no boundaries, they are often abused.

- Some people maintain barriers to communication and interaction. They do not want intimacy. Their relationships, if they have them, are superficial. The barriers keep people at a safe distance. They are afraid to allow people inside their borders. Their barriers protect the person from potential harm and disappointment, but they also prevent intimacy and growth. The person who lives behind the barriers becomes trapped inside. The barriers keep others out, but they keep him in. These people are lonely or they choose to be by themselves.

- People with a weak personal identity can have boundaries which are rigid and inflexible. To compensate for their lack of *Self* or their lack of confidence, they want to be in control of everything and everyone, hoping it will give them a sense of power and identity. Or, they may want to merge with the identity of the people around them. They may discourage their loved ones from growing into their own persons, for fear of being left alone. These people foster codependence.

- Some people are boundary violators. They do not respect the identity and boundaries of others. They do not have personal boundaries which can contain their own emotions and impulses. Their needs, their wants, their emotions erupt onto others and make people feel unsafe around them. The only relationships they can maintain are with people who are weak, vulnerable and have poor self-esteem. These people abuse others emotionally, physically, sexually and spiritually.

If we do not have healthy boundaries and a sense of our own identity, we will tend to attract people with the same problems. Both people in the relationship will desire love and intimacy, but they will be ill-equipped to achieve their goal. Their unhealthy boundaries will prevent intimacy.

Learning to set healthy boundaries and respecting the boundaries of the others is an important ingredient for establishing healthy relationships. Healthy boundaries are necessary for building trust, intimacy and healthy interdependence/independence.

Both partners must learn to develop this important skill. To do it, both of you must take time to evaluate the needs of your body, mind, emotions and spirit. Those of you who come from healthy families will have already experienced healthy boundaries. You will have a sense of your own identity and your boundaries. Because you have them, you will respect the individual identity and boundaries of your partner. With this basic trust, acceptance and safety, you will be able to establish an intimate relationship.

Those of you who come from unhealthy families with unhealthy boundaries will have a harder time. To assist you in the process of developing healthy boundaries, I will guide you through the following steps.

1. Become Aware of Your Own Identity and What Boundaries You Need

To assist yourself with understanding your individual identity, I highly recommend that you begin the practice of keeping what I call a **"holistic" Journal,** one that tracks the messages from your body, mind, emotions and spirit.

"Holistic" Journal

The length of the entries is not important. What is important is that you make consistent entries in your journal, over a long period of time. Don't worry about penmanship, grammar or composition.

What you are searching for is information about your *Self* — your feelings, how your body reacts to situations, your desires, your aspirations and dreams, your disappointments, your successes, your failures and how you cope with them, your fears, the ways you interact with people. If you write on a regular basis, you will get to know your *Self* and your truths.

A holistic Journal can become the "safe place" to learn to connect to your body, mind, emotions and spirit. It is the paradox of doing spiritual work that only when you are "strong enough," can you explore your "weakness." Only when you are humble enough to admit that you don't know yourself, can you find your true *Self*.

In your holistic Journal, you give yourself permission to listen to your body. Where are you holding pain, anxiety and anger? Where is your body tight? Where is the "codependent hole" — in your abdomen or your heart? Where do you hold sadness and despair? When you binge on food, is it because your body is hungry or is food trying to plug a hole or stuff a feeling? What is going on when you clinch or grind your teeth? What emotions do you anesthetize with drugs or alcohol, or being in a state of constant motion?

When you are feeling over-whelmed by emotions you cannot control or understand and are on the verge of a relapse or an outburst or feel that your only recourse is one of total withdrawal, you can begin writing in your Journal and trace the origin of the emotional response. Is this an issue from your childhood that has surfaced in your current relationship? Why do you feel so hurt or angry or disappointed by this person? Why are you feeling ashamed? Why are you filled with self-loathing? What are the longings of your spirit?

Once you know your *Self*, you will want to establish boundaries to protect your *Self*. In your Journal, you will be able to evaluate whether your current boundaries are healthy. You will see if they are too rigid or non-existent. You will learn that "one boundary style does not fit all occasions and all people." Sometimes you need more space and distance, other times you need less. With some people you need to erect a wall of protection because they are boundary violators.

When you track your interactions with other people in your Journal, you will be able to see if people feel safe around you or whether you violate their boundaries. Eventually, you will learn to make adjustments in your boundary style. As you learn this skill, you will begin to establish trust, which will lead to intimacy.

Long-Term Yoga Class

Another excellent way to become aware of your boundaries is by attending a yoga class over a period of time. For those of you who have difficulty defining your personal boundary or border — the energy field around your body which contains your mind, emotions and spirit — yoga class can be an excellent place to learn about it.

To begin with, when you enter a yoga class, you have to make a decision about where to place your mat. Do you want to place it close to another student or do you want a lot of space between you and the other students? The amount of space you choose is your first boundary.

When the class begins, the instructor will ask you to lie down on your mat and begin the warm-up exercises. You will be shown how to do deep abdominal breathing and how to relax every area of your body. In the quietness of the yoga studio, you will begin to hear the sounds of your breathing and learn to identify the various parts of your body where you hold stress and tension.

As you breathe and move through the various poses, you feel the circulation of energy — chi — moving through your muscles. You will become connected to your head, throat, shoulders, arms, hands, chest, abdomen, buttocks, thighs, ankles and feet. Your body temperature will increase as you stretch and move. Tension will be released and the muscles will elongate. Energy will travel through the various organs of your body: the heart, the lungs, the stomach, the intestines. The flow of this energy will make sounds in your abdomen and colon, helping your digestion, and it will strengthen your immune system.

As you continue the breathing and relaxation, you may become aware of various emotions and thoughts you are hold-ing in your mind and body. The breathing will decrease the intensity of these emotions and thoughts, making them "man-ageable." In the quiet and peacefulness of the yoga studio, you will get in touch with your spirit. You will gain a sense that your spirit can bring peace and hopefulness to your inner world and to your life.

Over time, you will become more and more aware of your individual identity — body, mind, emotions and spirit — and you will be ready to set boundaries for your *Self* and the people in your life.

Yoga provides other psychological benefits that will assist you with establishing healthy boundaries. With careful attention to your inner process as you practice the various poses, you will gain psychological insights about your *Self* and develop emotional, mental and spiritual strength. Let me give you some examples:

- **Standing poses.** With every part of your torso in alignment, you will learn balance and the ability to literally "stand on your own two feet." This awareness can be very powerful for a timid person. What you learn to do with your body can be transferred to other areas of your life. The timid person will learn to trust himself and will be inspired to establish boundaries.

- **Plank and downward facing dog poses.** In these poses you will strengthen your abdominal "core" — the muscles in your diaphragm, stomach, intestinal area, back. Your "core" is the central part of your body and it is the "house of your power." By strengthening this area, you will develop the power to stand up for your convictions and your boundaries.

- **Seated poses.** With straight or twisted spine, neck, head and shoulders lifted, face relaxed and serene, ebb and flow of oxygen in your lungs and abdomen, you will experience a sense of your own dignity and sovereignty. These are beautiful postures to behold. This new sense of yourself will transfer to your personal life. You will learn to carry yourself with dignity and establish healthy boundaries to protect yourself in relationships.

- **Prayer poses.** With palms together, elbows extended to the sides, hands resting gently in front of your heart, neck and head lifted, you will experience a state of serenity and a feeling of being "centered" in your body. When you feel centered, fear will diminish. When you are not afraid, you will not need rigid boundaries.

- **Poses which twist and bend the spine.** In order to twist or bend your spine, you must learn to "let go" in your muscles. As you twist or bend, the spine becomes more flexible, less rigid. Energy flows through your spine more easily, invigorating the other parts of your body. As you twist, your internal organs are gently massaged, releasing tension and aiding your digestion and immune system functioning. The increased flexibility of your spine will transfer to your emotional, mental, spiritual and social life. Patterns and boundaries that were rigid will become more flexible, allowing for a flow of energy, creativity and love in your life and your relationships.

2. Evaluate Your Current Boundary Style By Using the Following "Boundary Assessment" Tool

(Copy this Assessment tool and circle the parts which apply to you.)

Boundary Assessment Tool

I have healthy, flexible boundaries:

- I know my own identity and stand up for my needs and rights.
- I adjust my boundaries, according to the circumstances.
- I respect other peoples' boundaries and rights.

- When I experience stress, I go inside my *Self* and figure out what I need and am capable of providing it for myself.

I have unhealthy boundaries:

- I do not have a clear sense of my own identity.
- I have no boundaries.
- I put up protective barriers that shut other people out.
- I attempt to control others.
- I have no identity and tend to merge with others' identities.
- I am a boundary violator who ignores other peoples' identities and boundaries.
- I have trouble containing my own impulses and emotions and I violate others' boundaries.

Once you have completed this Assessment tool, you may notice that you have a mixture of healthy and unhealthy boundaries.

3. Attempt to Change Your Current Boundary Style to One That is More Healthy

Making this kind of change will be difficult. You probably adopted your current boundary style when you were a child. It is familiar to you and has become nearly an "automatic," default response. You may not even notice that you are doing it.

For this reason, I recommend working in Individual therapy. Your therapist will give you an objective view of your process and coach you on how to adopt a new style of boundaries. This transition will require time and a lot of work, but it will enhance the quality of your life with your *Self* and allow you to achieve intimacy in your relationships.

It is important for you to realize that when you change your boundary style, there will be repercussions. You and the people in your life are part of a "system." When there is a change in one part of the system, there will be a ripple effect to the other parts of the system. Let me give you some examples:

- For those of you who did not have boundaries and start using boundaries, the people in your life will become confused and sometimes angry. They can no longer "have their way" inside your borders. They are used to having you do what *they* want you to do. Over time, as you explain your new identity and your need for boundaries, they will either appreciate and respect you for becoming your own person or they will try to remove your boundaries or they will leave you. It's a risk, but one well worth taking. To have no identity or boundaries for the *Self* is far more painful and devastating than the loss of a relationship.

- For those of you who come out from behind your barriers, you will encounter feelings and situations you never experienced before. Initially, it will be scary. As you develop a secure identity, a process for handling your emotions, and reasonable boundaries to protect yourself, you will gain a sense of confidence and the ability to negotiate boundaries with the people in your life.

- For those of you who were boundary violators, you must learn that you cannot always have your way and that you must learn to contain and process your emotions and impulses. This will be very hard to do. It will require you to gain control over your impulsive Inner Child. You will also have to learn to respect other peoples' identities and boundaries.

- Don't get discouraged. As difficult as it will be to change, *it is possible!* As you change and become a safer person to be around, the people in your life will reward you with increased trust. As you establish trust with each other, you will be able to give and receive the love you so desperately crave. You will be blessed.

4. Discuss Boundaries With Your Mate and Work Together to Establish Healthy Boundaries

This needs to be an on-going process throughout the life of your relationship. Both of you will tend to operate from the boundary style you adopted as children. Indeed, you will notice a correlation between your boundary style and the coping mechanisms you used as a child.

It will be very difficult for you to see your own part in an unhealthy boundary style. The blessing here is that your partner, your spouse can give you objective feedback on what they observe and experience with you. You need to be open to those comments. Both of you may notice that you use the boundary style of your family of origin, with some original twists of your own. When you are giving feedback to each other, be gentle. Our boundary style can be a very touchy subject, laden with emotion and shame. The feedback you give should be kind and instructive; not harsh and condemning.

Once again, I highly recommend working together in couple's therapy. Your therapist will be able to give you his or her objective observation of how you interact with each other. The therapist will also coach you on how to make changes. Working together in an atmosphere of honesty, objectivity, trust and respect, you will learn to honor each other's individual identity and boundaries. You will enable yourselves to have the love and intimacy you both desire.

Keep in mind that in times of stress, you will both revert to your earlier boundary styles. Temporarily, you will become more rigid and unhealthy. When the stress abates and with proper reflection, your boundaries will become more flexible and healthy.

Chapter 27

THE "MARTIAL ART" OF FIGHTING FAIR

"You must understand the spectrum of anger and learn to become assertive."

~ J.D.

In the martial arts, there is a disciplined, focused use of energy. Anger, like love, is a strong emotion which generates a tremendous amount of energy. Unsupervised, it can be destructive and debilitating.

When we are growing up and in our lives as adults, no one teaches us about anger. Most people are afraid of their own or other peoples' anger. I believe we feel anger for three main reasons.

- When we are hurt or disappointed by others.

- When others do not do what we want them to do.
- When others have something we want but do not have, and we feel entitled to take it.

How we express our anger is dependent upon a variety of conditions.

- The manner in which our parents expressed anger.
- The coping mechanisms we learned as children.
- The amount of frustration tolerance and impulse control we have.
- The social mores of our sub-group.

I propose that there is a "global spectrum" of ways in which anger is expressed.

At one extreme are the **"passive" forms of anger:**

- Internalized anger: Anger is unexpressed in the outer world and is turned inward, on the *Self*, producing depression, disorders in the body, addictions and suicide.
- Sullen, withholding anger: Recognition, conversation, love are withheld in an attempt to punish.
- Crying: The person feels angry but does not feel "worthy" of expressing it.
- Whining: There is a nasal quality to the whining. It has been described as "anger coming out a small hole."

At the other extreme are the **"active" forms of anger:**

- Passive aggression and sarcasm: Here, the anger is expressed indirectly, in the form of verbal "jabs" or mean behavior.

- Martyr role: The martyr is controlling, does everything without allowing others to help and then complains.

- Rage: The anger is out of control and out of proportion to the situation. There is high voice volume, frightening face and various forms of physical, emotional, mental or sexual abuse.

- Crimes against humanity: Theft of possessions, re-sources, and identity, adultery, school massacres, road rage, domestic violence, murder, rape, genocide, wars and terrorism are examples.

In the middle of the spectrum are healthy methods of expressing anger, which I will demonstrate. For the time being, try to identify where you fall on the spectrum. More than likely, each person in the relationship will have different styles of expressing anger, which will be baffling to the other. To guide you in developing a healthy expression of anger, I will give you a "Don't List."

- **Don't use sarcasm.** Sarcasm is a passive aggressive form of anger. You hit the person in the stomach with your comment, at the same time you are wearing a smile on your face. The "victim" feels hurt and confused. You have given them a "double message" which is difficult to decipher. When confronted, you say, "But I was only kidding." You are not taking responsibility for your anger and the other person does not feel safe around you.

- **Don't hit below the belt.** As a couple, you are privy to each other's secrets, weaknesses, flaws and vulnerabil-ities. You should never use them when you fight, as you destroy trust and teach each other to hide vulnerability.

- **Don't use cruel or disrespectful words.** Profanity and demeaning phrases are attempts to control and demoralize the other person. It is your desire to elevate yourself by putting them down. When you do this, you degrade yourself and shame the other person. A relationship cannot grow in such an environment.

- **Don't "stock pile" past offenses.** When you are angry, express your feelings as soon as possible. Stick to the present circumstance. If you stock pile resentments and use them in your current argument, you will overwhelm the other person and shut down communication and resolution,

- **Don't project your own bad traits and motives onto your partner.** You must be aware of and own your conscious and unconscious feelings. If you do not, they become your "Shadow," which you are likely to project onto your partner.

- **Don't verbally assassinate your partner's family, children or pets.** Stick to the issues between the two of you. Express your feelings and needs and look for a resolution.

- **Don't violate the other person's physical, emotional, or psychological boundaries and need for safety.** You must learn to control your anger and your impulses. A person who acts out in rage is an adult whose Inner Child is running the show. The child is lost, frightened, overwhelmed or throwing a temper tantrum. The child might be replicating his parents' manner of dealing with anger, or else, he has bottled up wounds which have never been healed.

In my own experience, rage was a defense mechanism I learned in childhood. In my family, it was not safe to be vulnerable. I latched on to kicking and sarcasm at first, then moved to rage as defensive weapons for self-protection. "If I am strong, you cannot crush me." Unfortunately, the rage became the "cork on the bottle" which kept me from feeling the scary, vulnerable feelings inside the bottle. As an adult, when I was feeling overwhelmed, rage gave me a false sense of power, became the glue to hold my fragmenting pieces together and fueled me to muscle my way through difficult tasks.

Rage meets the criteria to be classified as an addiction. It is a mood altering behavior that has disastrous consequences. It violates the physical, emotional, mental and spiritual boundaries of your loved ones. It causes them to live in constant fear and feel unsafe in your presence, even in those times when you might be giving them love. It damages and wounds them on the deepest levels and impedes their ability to trust and bond with others.

The toll rage takes on you is equally disastrous. It is the behavior of a child. When you use rage, you rob yourself of the opportunity to become a healthy, mature adult. Rage destines you to remain a frightened, out-of-control child. A person who is a "rage-aholic" is filled with self-loathing, shame and guilt. These feelings only fuel more rage. Rage attacks are like volcanic eruptions. The steam and boiling lava are temporarily released, but are never completely emptied. The rage-aholic lives in constant fear of losing control. The Inner Child is trapped in a cycle of self-defeating behavior and never receives the love, self-esteem and safety he so desperately craves.

A rage addiction can be healed if the adult is willing to do the long, hard work. The adult must build a relationship with his Inner Child. He must help this child identify the wounds and vulnerable feelings of fear, sadness, loss and hurt and teach the child to express his or her feelings in an appropriate manner. The adult must set boundaries for the Inner Child and teach him to respect the rights and boundaries of others. The adult must provide a safe environment for the child and attend to his needs.

Once this is done, the adult will gain frustration tolerance, self-confidence, pride, and the ability to communicate, love and solve problems with the people in his life. The Inner Child will be released from his inner prison and will thrive in this new, safe environment — free to play, make friends and express his creativity.

"Rules of Engagement" for the Martial Art of Fighting Fair

1. **When you become aware that you are angry, take some time to be quiet with yourself.** Breathe slowly from your abdomen. Slow down your heart rate, listen to your body and try to locate where you are holding energy. Go to that part of your body and try to listen to your feelings. You might be holding anger in your jaw, your hands, your stomach, your back. You might be sitting on your anger and holding it in your buttocks or bowels. Anger might be choking your chest or vocal cords or causing you to grit your teeth.

    Hang out in your body for a while. Don't assume that you are only feeling anger. I guarantee there is something else going on. Continue the slow breathing and see what other feelings come to the surface. You may notice sadness, loneliness, disappointment in your heart. You may feel hurt or guilt or rejection in your gut. You may notice flushed cheeks that indicate you are feeling shame. Your mind might feel anxious, confused, frustrated or overwhelmed.

2. Once you have a clear picture of your anger and other vulnerable feelings, **ask yourself what or who caused or provoked your reaction.**

3. **Visualize how you want to resolve the situation.** Address the person or the situation as soon as possible. Don't avoid. Don't internalize. I suggest you begin your conversation with some "user friendly" comments:

    "I love you and appreciate what you have to say."
    "I love you very much and want our relationship to be healthy."

    No one will listen to you if you come in blazing and shoot them with accusations and insults. If you do that, they will close their ears, back into a corner and come out swinging.

    Once you have engaged the person, move to a calm discussion of the problem. Ask them to listen while you express your feelings, reactions and needs. Use "I" Statements: "I feel.......... I need........ I want........... I didn't like it when you........."

4. **Allow the other person time to assimilate what you have said.** Listen quietly as they express their feelings, reactions and needs. Encourage them to use "I" statements. If the other person begins blaming, insulting or abusing you, set and maintain your boundaries.

    "I am leaving the room if you are shouting."

"I will not subject myself to abuse."

"I am walking away. Let me know when you calm down."

If the other person is not able to respond, give them time to digest what you have presented. Do not violate their boundaries. Do not insist that they talk right now. Allow them time to get back to you. Learn to tolerate things being unresolved and "not okay." Many times there are conflicts and problems which cannot be fixed right away. Don't jump to the conclusion that a temporary impasse is impossible to resolve.

5. **Learn to take care of your own needs and wants when you are upset.** Find healthy ways to make yourself feel better. Exercise, meditation, journaling, prayer, warm baths and massage, gardening, talking to a friend, playing with your children or your pet are all ways to dissipate your anger and return your being to a state of peace. If the other person will not work with you to resolve the problem, take your own power and find a solution to the problem.

Chapter 28

MONEY MANAGEMENT:
The Ultimate "Hot Button"

An attempt to discuss money can ignite more heat and anger for a couple than even a discussion of sex. People treat their money as more sacred than their bodies. They are private about how much they have, how they spend it and how they manage it.

I think the importance of money can be attributed to the society in which we live. Today, a person's money reflects their power, their worth (financial and emotional), their status, their ability to control others, their ability to amass possessions. Our current society is also very "me" oriented. "It's all about 'me' and 'mine'." By contrast, in the Navajo culture, the emphasis is on the "collective we," not "me" and "I."

When two people come together and form a relationship and a marriage, they bring their individual experiences with money with them. Some people were raised with money and feel entitled to it. Others were raised poor and may feel unworthy of having it or are preoccupied with getting it. Some people are frugal. Others are impulsive and irresponsible. Others, still, strike a balance — being able to spend it wisely, with enjoyment, while also saving, investing and giving it away.

Recent financial statistics show that most Americans currently carry a debt of $10,000 - $25,000. Not long ago, that would have been unthinkable! Back then, people abhorred debt and were ashamed of it. Nowadays, it seems normal. Seduced by credit card companies, home equity loans, advertising, and a desire to appear wealthy, people carry debt on their credit cards, their homes and their cars. People file bankruptcy without blinking an eye. Possessions become the façade, the "persona" they project to society. Financial institutions are greedy and haven't the slightest compunction when people lose their homes, their cars, their possessions, their dignity from missed payments or upside down loans. Just as money conveys a sense of power, esteem and status, when you have no money or carry tremendous debt, the lack of money can carry shame and desolation.

Are you beginning to see why money management is such a touchy topic? It is a measure of one's self-esteem, competency and fluency. It is a report card. If you have money and manage it well, you want the entire world to know. If you have no money and carry extensive debt, you feel ashamed and are secretive. It's even worse when one partner in the relationship secretly spends the collective money and imposes debt, bad credit and humiliation on the fiscally responsible partner. This is such an egregious offense, causing such deep emotional pain and loss of trust, that the marriage will rarely survive.

Another interesting aspect in our society is the role of gender in relationship to money. In the old days, men had the jobs and earned the money and women stayed home to raise the kids and manage the household. Because the men made the money, they generally controlled it. The wife might have written checks for the bills, but the husband controlled the accounts and told the wife what she could or could not spend. Wives tended to be obedient, but might have secretly stashed grocery or household money away, for their own spending. Some men made it clear it was "their" money and the wives were lucky to get some of it.

Financial institutions, corporations, courts, and family inheritance practices, which favored male heirs, also maintained the power in men's hands. It was humiliating, demeaning, and crippling for women. Although times have changed in terms of women in the work force and women in some high executive positions, there is still a "glass ceiling" and much of the discrimination remains in place. Men still earn a higher salary for doing the very same job a woman does at a lower salary. Men feel more empowered to ask for raises and incentives and are much more likely to receive them than their female counterparts.

In most relationships, I think men still think they should control the money or have the final say. Huge battles are fought when the women want to share the power and decision making. Occasionally the roles are reversed, where the woman is the bread winner or earns the higher salary and the man stays home or earns less. When I work with these couples, I often see battles for control or issues with self-esteem. Often, the women are controlling and condescending and the men feel maligned and impotent.

How We Learn to Handle Money

How we earn and manage our money is also highly influenced by how our parents handled money. I will give some examples:

♦ Many people were raised in families where there was a shortage of money and resources, utilities were often turned off for failure to pay, parents constantly fought or worried over money and the children felt frightened and ashamed. These same children turned into adults who feel unworthy to have money and are unskilled in handling what they have.

♦ Most families do not discuss money management with their children. The children do not witness and learn how their parents balance a budget or reconcile their check books. When children do not learn these skills, they become prey to the salesmen from credit card companies that seduce them on high school and college campuses, promising "instant ability to spend," while concealing the small print implications about late payments and interest rate penalties.

♦ Children who are raised by parents who own their own businesses might be more prepared to handle money, if they are educated about the business and given legitimate jobs. Many times they are being groomed to be the eventual owners.

♦ As a rule of thumb, however, I would say that most people do not appreciate what is given too freely, without their need to work for it. If the parents are wealthy and enable their children to purchase whatever they want, with no responsibility to budget or earn it, these children will feel entitled to money and privileges and be disinclined to earn or budget their money as adults. These very same adults might have emotional breakdowns or unrelenting battles with their spouses if they lose their money, status or power in the course of their marriage. Many "trust fund babies" fall into depression as adults because they lack the self-esteem garnered from hard work and discipline.

♦ Children, who were raised in poor families and were forced to get jobs at an early age and pay their own way through college, are often quite mature, humble and capable when it comes to managing money. Their hard work has given them pride and self-confidence and the ability to postpone gratification. Immigrants to America are often focused, hard working and responsible with their money. They value their money, yet choose to be responsible for their family members.

Examples of Money Management Problems

♦ Some adults enter a relationship with a covert expectation and demand to be taken care of. They are wanting to replicate their "child role" from their enabling family of origin. They secretly have no intention of working and want no restraints on the ability to spend the partner's earnings. These intentions might be hidden during the courtship, but become painfully obvious during the marriage. The unsuspecting partner is blind sided and becomes angry and resentful.

♦ I can easily say that disagreements, quarrels and power struggles over money contribute to a high percentage of divorces. Once people are divorced, there are a whole new set of problems.

Everyone suffers financially and emotionally in a divorce. Men are angry that they lose the family home and are required to pay child support, at least, and sometimes alimony as well. Women are angry if they lose the family home and have to move into an apartment, trying to raise the children with only one income. Many times, they have to go to court to have their child support order enforced. Children of divorced parents hear the war stories about court battles over money and child support. Divorced adults become embittered, attached to the money they have and apprehensive about someone taking it away or telling them how to manage it. Children of divorced parents often grow up afraid to get married.

♦ Another problem with money management pertains to those people who have compulsive spending or gambling addictions — which result in disastrous consequences. These mood altering behaviors are attempts to escape internal pain or to experience a "rush" or euphoria or a feeling of social potency. The spending and gambling provide temporary relief or excitement, but, like with an alcoholic, "one drink is never enough." The person promises himself he will stop gambling or she will stop spending, but they are driven to repeat the behavior.

The "substance of choice" (compulsive spending or gambling) becomes their preoccupation and the center of their life. The addiction takes over and the person loses control of reason and restraint. At some point, these people experience the disaster phase of their addiction, where they lose their jobs, their money, their homes, their families and their paltry amount of self-esteem. A cycle of addiction ensues, where the person needs more and more of the "substance of choice" to escape the compounding levels of depression and self-loathing.

Bombarded by seductive ads for alcohol, package deals offered by casinos, cable programs featuring professional gamblers, movies romancing the exciting events at casinos, internet gambling and shopping, and state lotteries and race tracks, it is no wonder many people succumb to this form of addiction.

Learning to Manage Your Finances Successfully

Learning to manage your money in a responsible manner is an essential skill for a couple. Whatever your background as a child and experience as an adult, you can learn to work together and produce good results. Remember that you are a couple, attempting to establish a healthy marriage between two very different individuals. The process will, no doubt, be frightening and daunting. **But be of good cheer, it can be done.** You must be patient and gentle with one another. Financial stability is a key element in the foundation of a marriage.

Think of this process as starting a corporation together. The two partners must have a common vision and mission statement and they must have the funds to finance the operation.

Both partners will be executive officers and operation officers. Both must be informed and each must work with the other in order to be successful.

Here are some guidelines for the healthy management of your money:

1. **Begin with full financial disclosures.** Whether you are engaged or already married, I recommend an initial, as well as on-going, disclosure of the following:
   - your salary
   - your checking account balance
   - your savings account balance
   - your debt (credit cards, loans)
   - your credit report and credit score
   - your financial obligations (child support and alimony)
   - your 401K and investments

   Property and possessions you own prior to your marriage are your own assets. Inheritances remain your own private asset. Debts that you have prior to the marriage are your own. Debts and credit ratings that you accumulate during the marriage, bought with "commingled funds," become the liability of the couple.

   I know that this kind of disclosure is scary, but there can be no "secrets" or "withholds." My husband and I did not have the courage to make these disclosures during our engagement, therefore, it caused substantial amounts of pain and conflict later. We had been afraid that the financial facts would prevent us from going forward into the marriage. We proceeded into the marriage "with our heads in the sand," but the problems did not go away. They only magnified. Eventually, we had to make the disclosures.

Too bad we hadn't done it earlier. A lot of anger, resentment and heartache could have been prevented.

Each partner has the right to know about the other and the obligation to put the facts on the table. Remember, you are forming a corporation and you have to know the assets and the debts.

2. **Discuss your financial goals as a couple.** If there are debts, I recommend that each person be responsible to clear their own debt. If one pays off the debt of the other, the person with the debt does not learn responsibility and the ability to postpone gratification in the future.

   When you pay off your own debts, you learn from your mistakes, gain a sense of pride in accomplishment, and make wiser fiscal decisions. I do not recommend filing bankruptcy, except in the most extreme circumstances. Many who file bankruptcy remain irresponsible and are likely to pile up more debt. Organize your financial goals into categories: Present and Future.

3. **Decide what kind of banking accounts you want to set up.** There are many different options. Engaged couples will more than likely maintain their own separate accounts during the engagement, then switch to joint accounts when they get married. People who have been divorced and are re-marrying might prefer to keep separate accounts and one joint account. Married couples who are reading this might want to re-evaluate their current accounts and make some changes. My husband and I keep our own separate accounts, but contribute equally to joint expenses.

4. **Sit down together and create a budget** for maintaining your household expenses, entertainment, obligations and saving plans. This should not be a "one person" process. Both of you must be in agreement and both of you have an ongoing responsibility to be involved. I highly recommend that each partner have some monthly "discretionary money" for their own needs and interests. Having some personal money makes life fun and rewarding. We all need to spend some money on ourselves.

   The key to a budget is **Balance**. You must balance fixed expenses, entertainment, big ticket purchases and improvements, savings, obligations, payment of debt, and a "cushion" for emergencies and unexpected events. To achieve balance, you must exercise discipline and reason.

5. **Share with each other how you have managed money in the past and how your parents handled money.** Your partner will be a lot more patient and understanding if you are open about your history as a child and your experiences as an adult. Don't be afraid to admit a lack of knowledge about how to balance a check register or bank statement. If you do not have this skill, ask for help from your partner or ask for assistance from a bank officer. If you were raised by parents who were irresponsible or controlling with their money, work with your partner to be different than your parents.

6. **Decide who is going to pay the monthly bills.** Again, I don't think this should be a "one person operation." If one of you is more skilled as an accountant or bookkeeper, the role could easily fall to you. The problem with one person writing the checks is that the other person does not acquire that skill. Another problem is that the "bill payer" might

end up worrying more about the money, while the one who doesn't write the checks is in their own plastic bubble; spending mindlessly, unaware of the balances in the accounts.

There should be an ongoing dialogue about the budget, bills and bank balances. Credit cards can cause problems because they encourage us to spend money we don't have, without consideration of consequences. Using ATM cards and not entering the withdrawals in a check register can result in bounced checks.

As a couple, be aware of the number of credit cards you have and the interest rates you are paying. **Pay your bills on time!** Missed payments, late payments, and astronomical interest rates and penalties can result in foreclosures, poor credit ratings and low credit scores, liens against your property and debts that are hard to clear. In addition, file your income tax reports on time. You might want to consult an accountant about whether you should file "Married, filing separate" or "Married, filing jointly." Work together with financial institutions to consolidate your debt and reduce your interest rates.

7. **Periodically, review your financial goals as a couple and the reality of your spending.** If your spending is out of line with your goals, make some adjustments! Don't lapse into denial, only to blame each other for misfortune in the future.

8. **Educate yourself about finances.** There are many opportunities for learning: seminars, books and tapes, money management programs on Public Broadcasting, financial consultants, bank officers and stock brokers. Learning

about money, protecting your money and growing your money can be fun.

9. **Protect your family's future.** All of us are afraid to contemplate the possibility of death, but it is something that will happen to all of us. I highly recommend facing your fears and deciding how you can responsibly protect your family in the future. Make decisions about beneficiaries on accounts and retirement plans. Consider life insurance policies. Take the time to have a Will drawn up. Decide if you want to establish some sort of trust. Discuss your feelings about funeral arrangements. Consider establishing a medical power of attorney, in the event you become incapacitated.

Once again, these are scary topics, but ones well worth discussing. When you marry, you are called to be responsible for yourself and the other person. Making these arrangements does not hasten your demise. They simply relieve you of the speculation and bless your family. They give you a sense of pride and satisfaction in taking good care of your family.

Chapter 29

SEX
When Does it Become "Love Making"?

Adiscussion of sex is a humbling undertaking. As a woman and a therapist, I think this is the hardest topic to articulate. Sex is a subject which has inspired and baffled writers, poets, artists, philosophers, film makers, song writers and the common man worldwide. It is complex, complicated, multi-faceted and somewhat paradoxical. It is something men, women and animals were designed to do. Yet, how can something which is so straight forward physically be so hard to grasp?

I think the answer is that sex is so much more than physiological. I believe that for humans, it was designed to be mental, emotional and spiritual as well. I would say that sex becomes "love making" when two conditions are met:

- there is a union of the body, mind, emotions and spirit of the two people

- the needs of the other person become more important than our own.

Exploring How Our Feelings About Sex are Formed

Before you can understand this concept, I think we need to explore how our feelings about sex are formed. Whether or not we enjoy sex and become capable of "making love" is influenced by our childhood, our parents, our religion in many cases, our culture, our history of sexual encounters, our self-esteem, our body image, our ability to trust, the functioning of our sexual organs, and finally, our connection to our spirit and ourselves.

- **Growing up,** we are given a variety of messages about sex. If our parents were loving and affectionate with one another, we absorb a non-verbal message that touch, affection and even sex are normal and good. Children sense that their parents' bedroom is a special, sacred place. They do not see the sex, but they sense that something mysterious goes on in the bedroom, in the bed, between the parents. Even our pets sense it. I think that's why children and pets love to come into their parents' bed.

    A good feeling about eventual sex is absorbed by children if they see that their parents are happy. If children see laughter, respect, kindness, affection, admiration, the acceptance of sex will be laid in the foundation of the young psyche. When the time comes to experience sex, these children will be ready to enjoy it.

    Many children, however, are not raised by parents who paint a good picture of love or sex. In these households, children see fear and intimidation, anger and

319

resentment, coldness and bitterness, ridicule, lack of affection and respect, and, in some cases, physical and sexual abuse and incest. Many of the adults who come to me for therapy have been molested or sexually abused as children; by family members, friends of the family, neighbors, teachers and clergy. These experiences leave an indelible mark on the psyche, body, emotions and spirit.

Children's sexual esteem is also influenced by their parents' reaction to sexual exploration. It is normal for small children to touch and stimulate their sexual organs. It is normal for them to explore other children's bodies. If this innocent behavior is met with shock, anger, shame and punishment, children get the message that their sexual organs are shameful and bad. If children show signs of homosexuality and are treated with disgust or disdain by their parents, these children will grow up with sexual confusion and self-loathing. If children do not receive love and attention from their parents, they may turn to masturbation and early sexual activity for self-soothing and comfort. This behavior can become compulsive and addictive.

- **Teenagers continue to be influenced by their family.** If they are shamed for the development of their sexual characteristics (breasts, pubic hair, menstruation, widening of hips for girls; wet dreams, chest, facial and pubic hair, and changing of their voice for boys), the teenagers will feel ashamed of their bodies. If they are raised in families with strict fundamentalist religious beliefs, these teenagers may pick up the message that sex and the human body are bad. Excessive and rigid parental control of dating, dancing, and clothing can make teenagers feel guilty about their natural sexual urges and desires to date. They may surmise that sex is bad and that the opposite sex is to be feared. Or they may rebel against their parents and secretly get sexually involved, while feeling guilty about it. By contrast, lack of parental guidance and boundaries can propel teenagers into early sexual activities.

- **Our current society's fascination and preoccupation with sex** — in advertising, clothing, television, internet, movies, bill boards, music videos — and the deterioration of family structure and stability have resulted in teenagers becoming sexually active at earlier ages. It is fairly common for fourteen year olds to be sexually active.

  Our current society also gives teenagers some alarmingly negative messages about sex. Child and adult pornography Web sites demean the dignity of sex and the human body. Rap songs demean and objectify women. Date rape has become common on many college campuses and is often denied by fraternities, sports teams and campus administrators. Women who are raped are often maligned by police, the press and lawyers.

- **The sexual experiences we have as teenagers and young adults influence how we will perceive sex in marriage.** Once again, it is a complicated phenomenon. I'm sure we can all remember the first time we had sex. For boys, it is a sense of accomplishment and pride. They are excited to tell their peers and are relieved that their "equipment" worked. For girls, it is infinitely more complicated. The first intercourse for a girl is painful. The hymen is broken and the vagina might not be prepared for penetration. There may be blood and pain. There is the possibility and fear of pregnancy. There is

321

the question of the girl's "reputation." There is the reaction of the parents. There is a sense of accomplishment or the relief of "getting it over." There is the question, "Is that it? I thought it was going to be a lot more special than it was."

Then, for the teenagers, there is the question: "If we are having sex, do we need to be boyfriend and girlfriend?" Sometimes boys want to have a relationship. Many times they do not. For them, sex is exciting, and they want more of it with many different partners. Girls, on the other hand, tend to get attached with their hearts to their sexual partners. Girls, for the most part, are looking for more than sex. They are looking for affection, connection, love, safety and approval. They want to hear that their body is attractive, desirable and satisfying and that they are desirable, too.

The different needs of the boys and girls in regard to sex can set up a sticky dynamic. Boys enjoy sex. They are tactile and visual creatures. They easily can be aroused and turned on by sexual images, girls' clothing and the smell and touch of soft feminine skin and hair, and the allure of hips and breasts and vaginas. They want to have sex, plain and simple. They do not need to be in love or in a relationship.

Girls learn to be seductive with boys and spend hours on their hair, make up, clothing and appearance. They are generally interested in boys and want to have a boyfriend. In terms of sex, they may enjoy it or may simply go along with sex in order to get male attention. Girls who do not have a good relationship with their fathers and their mothers generally search for love, comfort and approval from a boy, at any price. They will risk pregnancy, endure humiliation and abuse, all in pursuit of being in a relationship.

The opposing needs and goals of girls and boys can set them at cross purposes with one another. Boys want sex and sometimes a relationship. Girls almost always want a relationship. In order to get their needs met, boys and girls can set up "false" relationships; where the boy promises he is in love, in order to get sex, and the girl promises or allows sex so she can have a relationship. This sets up the dynamic of "sexual tension." Sometimes the needs of both parties are satisfied. Often, they are not. Boys can be angry at girls for withholding or withdrawing sex. Girls can feel used and abused. These young, impressionable boys and girls can have their hearts broken or their psyches severely damaged. Sometimes it's the boy who wants love and the girl who is using him for her purposes, then dumps him.

Some boys and girls experience their first, serious love as teens. This first love is innocent and quite beautiful. It is an opportunity for the touching of bodies and spirits, romantic dreams and powerful emotions. It is an attempt to find and experience love outside their parents' home, on the journey of self-discovery and emancipation. If this first love is a positive experience, it will facilitate finding more loving relationships in the future.

There is also the category of teenagers who do not get the opportunity to date and have sex. They may be excluded because of their race, their weight, their income, their looks, their disability, their not being in the right clique or any other variety of reasons. These kids experience deep heartache and sense of exclusion. They are prone to depression, self-loathing, addictions, acting out against society, suicide, and, in extreme cases, hate crimes and school massacres.

Then there are the cases of teenage girls or boys who are gay or lesbian. Often, they must date partners of the same sex in secret or participate in "pseudo hetero-sexual" dating in order to avoid social disapproval, potential rejection by their families, scorn from their peer group and fear of being physically attacked by people who hate them. For some, these compromises to dating are intolerable, so they don't date at all and are left feeling lonely and isolated. For this group of teen-agers, the evolution of the true *Self* is severely chal-lenged because society does not approve of them and they, in turn, often do not love or approve of themselves. There are thousands of gay and lesbian teenagers who suffer in silence, unknown to the general public. This is tragic.

In the teenage years, both boys and girls can accum-ulate negative feelings about sex and the opposite sex. Too many bad experiences can result in anger, distrust, disappointment and paranoia. Some boys develop such rage and disrespect for girls that they rape, abuse and objectify women later in their lives. Some girls become so disillusioned and bitter about boys that they become angry, cold, manipulative women who use and discard men. Some boys and girls decide to never have a rela-tionship. Some boys who are confused about their own sexuality get into "gay bashing" — punishing gays for the very tendencies they are afraid exist inside them-selves.

- **In young adulthood,** the feelings about love and sex continue to evolve. By this point, most people are looking for love and companionship. They have moved out of their parents' home and are feeling lonely. After graduation from school, it is harder to find people to date. Isolated and desperate, people turn to clubs and the internet to find partners. At clubs, the emphasis is on "hooking up" — sex without a relationship. Fueled by alcohol or drugs, many young adults make unwise, risky selections and end up more bruised and disillusioned. They might have also acquired sexually transmitted diseases and unwanted pregnancies. They are looking for love, but settle for "recreational sex" or one night stands. Whatever sexual complexes they carry from childhood and teen years are reinforced by more negative experiences.

After enough bad experiences, people can turn on themselves and begin to doubt their own desirability. Fueled by society's preoccupation with being thin, sexy and young, women might develop eating disorders or run to plastic surgeons to get their breasts, lips, cheeks, buttocks and wrinkles plumped or undesirable fat sucked from their bodies. Men can develop compulsive addictions to food, sex, gambling, drugs and alcohol and power.

People can spend years in unhealthy, codependent relationships because they are afraid to be alone. Failed marriages compound the damage, resulting in desperation, bitterness, and a promise to "never let someone hurt me again."

Many young peoples' bodies become "pressure cookers" — filled with desires for love and sex, feelings

of self-loathing, anger, sadness, loneliness and pessimism about ever finding love and a happy marriage.
Desperation can set in, which propels them into another
round of unhealthy dating and a back lash of hurt and
sorrow.

Recipe for a Healthy Sexual Relationship

Ever since childhood, we are looking for our basic needs for love
and approval to be provided in a safe environment. But our
experiences are often so hurtful that we cannot trust and we
become defensive and self-centered. We are often disconnected
from our own body, mind, emotions and spirit. We want to find
love and enjoy sex, but we are not capable of making love. We
have sex, but we do not make love.

I don't think we can grow into capable, generous sexual
partners until we feel safe and connected within and until we are
in a safe, monogamous relationship. Marriage provides the
perfect opportunity for healing, love and growth. Finally, after all
the years of searching, we have someone who truly loves and
accepts us. Finally, we have someone who is committed to us.
Finally, we can let go of our preoccupation with the *Self* and
concentrate on the needs and enjoyment of the other. Finally, we
can learn to "make love" and experience all the components of
sex coming together; a union of body, mind, emotions and spirit.

Marriage provides the opportunity, but it does not guarantee that the transformation will occur. I think most of us
come to marriage as children; we want to be loved and cared for,
we want to be gratified and we want life to be easy. Our first
thought is ourselves. **In order to become adults, we must learn
to think of the other person and turn love into an "action"**

word. What are the needs and desires of my partner? How can I care for him or her? How can I make sex more enjoyable? We must be willing to do the hard work of transforming ourselves from child to adult.

To guide you in this process, I will make some recommendations:

1. Honor your partner's body at all times. Never make fun of it. Never abuse it. Respect their boundaries.

2. Honor your partner's past. Take time to learn about their childhood and teenage years. Be gentle and patient with their sexual hang ups and wounds.

3. When you want to have sex, indicate it to your partner, but never demand sex or punish them for saying "no."

4. Don't use orgasm as the "criteria for success." Concentrate on the "process" of making love. Enjoy the touch, taste, smell, stimulation, bonding and relaxation.

5. Talk to each other about your sexual likes and dislikes. If your partner is stumbling to please you and can't quite figure out what you want or what will work, guide them along. If they do something you dislike or that hurts you or makes you feel uncomfortable, tell them.

6. Find ways to nurture your partner's body, mind, emotions and spirit. Massage, shared baths, great food, sensual atmosphere, thoughtful gifts and notes, weekend getaways, hugs, kisses, holding hands, long walks, phone calls and attentive listening are all forms of "making love."

7. Each of you should take responsibility for maintaining your own body, mind, emotions and spirit with exercise, healthy

327

diet, rest and relaxation and personal growth. A vital person is sexually attractive to others.

8. Forgive each other's shortcomings and encourage each other's growth. Don't try to have sex when you are angry.

9. Understand the "cycles" of love making. Frequency and intensity ebb and flow and are influenced by fatigue, diet, stress, drugs and alcohol, moods, time availability, demands of work and children, sickness, losses and aging.

10. Take responsibility to prevent unwanted pregnancies. Don't put yourself in the position of contemplating abortion as a method of birth control

If each of you focus on the other, your own needs will be met.

Taking Care of Our Bodies as We Age

Maintaining our bodies and our sex appeal throughout our marriage is a challenge. Bodies that are firm, muscular and slim in the twenties begin to change in the thirties and forties. Both men and women tend to gain abdominal girth as they age. Many women experience changes in their bodies after child birth.

Aging and gravity take their toll on all of us. Muscles, breasts, chins, skin, buttocks begin to sag. Hair is lost. Metabolism slows down, causing a tendency to gain weight. To maintain our weight, we must exercise more and eat wiser and smaller portions. By the fifties and sixties, it is even a greater challenge. The exercise routine that maintained you in your thirties and forties will no longer do the job. You must exercise longer, harder and smarter to maintain the body you want. Joints begin to break down, cartilage and bone density diminish, vertebrae and spinal discs compress. Women enter menopause and men experience diminished levels of testosterone and erectile functioning.

Yoga and Pilates can help people of all ages maintain core strength, spinal and muscular flexibility, deep breath relaxation, connection to spirit and general sense of well being.

War, injuries, accidents, illness, chronic medical conditions and surgeries also change our bodies. Sometimes the effects are minor, often they are significant, and sometimes they are profound. For people who have too much of their self-esteem tied up in their body image, the effect can be tragic. Sometimes people commit suicide because they cannot tolerate an amputation caused by diabetes or a war injury or because they become confined to a wheelchair. Sometimes women who have breast cancer and undergo mastectomies and hair loss are rejected by their husbands and fall into deep depressions.

It is important for each of us to love our own body and the body of our partner, throughout our lifetime. Our body is the temple for the mind, emotions and spirit. It is the house for the adult and the Inner Child. We must learn to be humble about the parts of our body we cannot change and work hard to change and maintain what we can. We must love and support our partner despite changes in their body and hope that they will do their own work to maintain what they have. If we are able to do this, we should have good sexual esteem and a good sexual relationship throughout the marriage.

If we do not, we may stumble during mid-life crises and "jump ship" to another relationship, another marriage to find what we do not have within. Many originally healthy marriages break under the strain and are lost. The new relationships or marriages which seemed promising may not deliver to our expectations, and we may be left with disappointment and loneliness.

One last point on the topic of the body. It is important for each of the partners to take responsibility for preventive medical, dental and visual care. Women should have yearly breast exams and pap tests, as well as routine physicals that include blood work and cholesterol tests. When they reach forty, they should have annual mammograms. By fifty, they should go for their first colonoscopy and have a baseline bone density test.

Men should have yearly physicals and blood work, paying close attention to cholesterol levels, heart functioning and blood pressure. By fifty, they should have manual prostate exams, PSA levels monitored, and their first colonoscopy. Many life threatening illnesses can be detected and treated during these routine exams, preventing unnecessary deaths and extending the lifetime of the couple.

SECTION EIGHT

A Spiritual Perspective

*"Your spirit is designed to lead you
to higher levels of growth."*

~ J.D.

Chapter 30

God/Higher Power

"Harnessing the Power that can resolve any impasse and nurture any relationship."

~ J.D.

I would like to propose that you consider the possibility of God or Higher Power and that you find some way to incorporate spirituality into your marriage. Why, you may ask? Isn't the power of the husband and wife sufficient? Can't we learn the skills to handle our own marriage? Aren't we the masters of our own destiny? What if we don't believe in God? What if we got turned off to religion by our experiences with our family?

These are all reasonable questions. People have struggled with them since the beginning of time. I realize that this is a touchy subject. The idea of God and religion has sparked wars throughout the world and has caused countless numbers of people to die. On the other hand, God and religion have also comforted people and inspired them to do great, selfless works to benefit mankind.

For our purposes, I would like to distinguish between three concepts:

- God/Higher Power
- Religion
- Spirituality

I would define **God/Higher Power** as a "Supernatural Force For Good" that loves us and wants us to achieve abundance in every area of our lives. I do not think it is important what we call this Force. Every religion in the world has their own name for it and indigenous people believe it resides in nature.

I further believe that the Force gives us the "right of self determination." We have the right to run our own lives, make our own decisions and be the center of our own universe. The Force loves us, yet will not violate our boundaries. It will not enter our lives unless we issue an invitation. It stands outside the door to our heart and waits, for an opportunity to enter and help us.

Religion, on the other hand, is a man made institution. It contains a specific ideology, a set of rules, people who run it and administer it, certain rites and buildings where people can gather to worship. Each religion has a belief that their approach to God and life is "the right way" and, in some cases, "the only way." Each religion is run by human mortals, who have strengths and weaknesses. Because it is a collection of human beings, it is fallible. Sometimes religions do great good. Sometimes they do great harm.

Spirituality can be defined as our own individual spirit making a connection to God or Higher Power. It is a personal relationship. It does not require a building, a dogma, a set of rules. It is, simply, the *Self* connecting to the Force. Our spirits get a glimpse of the Force when we are in the process of creating. Our spirits hear a voice, an inspiration deep within us that inspires us to create songs, music, art, writing, dance, movies and dreams. We experience the majesty of the Force when we commune with nature or give birth to our children or play with our pets. We are a conduit for the Force when we reach out to love and care for people, animals and the environment.

The Force has a power that is greater than our own. It has a vision that encompasses the past, the present and the future. In times of great need, It provides a strength that can surpass any limitation, any impasse. It provides us with a sense of peace that cannot be explained. The peace is felt in the heart center and it quiets our body, mind and emotions, despite the reality of our external circumstances. The peace does not come from man or the natural world. It is Supernatural.

Marriage to another human being is a challenging under-taking. Because of the inherent differences between a man and a woman, different families of origin, different cultures and life experiences, it is almost guaranteed to fail. The words in the old fashioned wedding ceremonies give us a glimpse of what we will encounter along the way:

- Sickness and health
- Richer and poorer
- Good times and bad

At the time we marry, none of us can see the future. We marry because we are in love and because we are optimistic. We have goals and dreams and we hope that our marriage will help us achieve them. In the course of our marriage, however, life will throw many unforeseen challenges and obstacles our way. We will experience hardships of every kind — financial, physical, mental and emotional. We and our loved ones will come under attack. There will be losses of every kind, heartache, financial reversals, life threatening illnesses, accidents, devastating acts of nature, plane crashes, auto accidents, wars and unexpected deaths.

There will come a time in each person's life when external and internal pressures and circumstances exceed our ability to cope. In those dire times, we have limited recourse:

- We can have a mental and emotional breakdown.
- We can develop an addiction, as a means of escape.
- We can ask for human help, which is finite.
- We can physically harm ourselves or someone else.
- We can call on God, who is Infinite.

I am suggesting to you that you call on God or Higher Power to help you when you cannot help yourselves and when human help is not available or is insufficient for the situation. Issue the invitation. Open the door to your heart. Make your needs known.

In my experience, there is not a situation beyond the reach of God's Power. When you invite God to enter your life and your marriage, you will experience the power of the Creator of the Universe. This power can turn darkness into light, despair into hope and transformation. This power can heal broken hearts, retrieve lost dreams, overcome illness, save marriages, protect our loved ones, open the doors to opportunity and growth, heal old wounds and guide us to achieve our highest good.

When I say "call on God or Higher Power," I am not suggesting that you become religious or that you even have a specific notion of what God is. In the Twelve-Step program it is explained, "Came to believe that there was a power greater than ourselves...." I am saying to you, if you do not believe in God, suspend your disbelief and ask for help anyway. Admit that you are powerless and that you are open to the possibility of a Higher Power, outside yourself, that can help you. It's that simple.

From that point forward, keep your eyes and ears open and watch for change to occur. Dr. Wayne Dyer speaks about the "power of intention" and "connecting to the Source." Connecting to God helps the intentions of our body, mind, emotions and spirit become manifest, through our energy and the Infinite Source of energy.

A relationship with God does not prevent our ultimate death. We are all going to die. But it can produce miraculous events. Countless people are "miraculously cured" of life threatening illnesses. Injured, stranded individuals have called on God and survived. Addicts whose lives were shattered and shackled by addictions have been transformed. Marriages that were doomed to divorce have been saved. The power of God can change the circumstances of our lives and help us achieve the desires of our hearts. It can bless you and every member of your family.

Chapter 31

FORGIVENESS
A "Spiritual" Skill That
We Need to Acquire

*"Our ability to forgive others is in direct proportion
to our ability to admit our own wrong doing
and to forgive ourselves."*
~ J.D.

I believe each of us is born with an innate desire to experience love and harmony in our relationships.

As humans, we are designed to be social beings and are destined to spend our lives in a series of relationships. We are interdependent. Each of us begins our life as our parents' child. In the course of our lifetime, we have many other relationships — siblings, family members, friends, lovers, co-workers, neighbors. Many of us become marriage partners, parents and grandparents.

Each of these relationships is fraught with the potential for harm, disappointment and hurt, as well as love, joy and great satisfaction. We may experience the full range of emotions within our relationships — happiness, love, peace, joy, sadness, betrayal, disappointment, resentment, anger, to name a few. The more important the relationship, the greater the intensity of the feelings.

This chapter is concerned with the problems that occur when things go wrong in relationships. Sometimes we are hurt or violated by others. Other times, we are the ones who hurt or violate. We do not do this with intention. We do it because we are human and we are limited.

Each of us is challenged in our relationships. We all have to deal with hurt and resentment. We all will be guilty of wrong doing. The redemptive aspect of our relationships is that they afford us the opportunity to learn and grow in our capacity to love.

Resentment or anger is a natural feeling we get when someone hurts or violates us. It is a protective reaction from the *Self.* When we are hurt or wronged by someone, the pain and disappointment are so great that we want to strike back and hurt the other person. We want to stand up for our *Self.* Even if we retaliate, we are inclined to hold on to the resentment, in the form of a grudge.

Resentment is a very strong emotion. It generates a great deal of energy and activates the stress hormones in the body. The body becomes poised, ready for action, in a state of alert. If it is not released, the body must contain the energy, hormones and the angry state of mind. Over time, these can be quite destructive to the body, mind and spirit. Resentment is so strong that it can over-power and dominate the other emotions.

Another problem with resentment is that it keeps the memories of the hurtful event alive within us. If we do not let go of hurt and resentment, we will continue to experience them, long after the event has past. The hurt, the anger, the resentment will continue to cycle throughout the body and the unconscious — leaving us in a state of exhaustion and depression. Sometimes, we further victimize ourselves by replaying the hurtful memory, over and over. When we do that, the suffering and resentment are intensified.

If we do not let go, we remain hostage to the event. Hurt and resentment, not released, will affect our bodies, minds, emotions and spirits.

What I am proposing to you in this chapter is that **forgiveness is the key that unlocks the door to our hearts, frees our bodies of hurt, resentment and guilt and enables us to achieve reconciliation and inner peace.** Forgiveness will also strengthen our immune systems, eliminate toxic build up and help prevent the development of life threatening illnesses.

I think forgiveness is one of the hardest skills to acquire because it goes against our base, human nature. When we are hurt, our natural inclination is to strike back. That is why I call it a "spiritual" skill.

"To err is human, to forgive is divine." The Bible and other holy books give so many references and teachings about forgiveness because it is an essential ingredient for healing and well being. Without forgiveness, all our relationships with others and our relationship with our *Self* will be compromised. When we are filled with guilt or shame, resentment or anger, we cannot experience love and abundance in our relationships.

Forgiveness doesn't erase the event, but it does heal the wound. **When you forgive the person who hurt you or wronged you, you are allowing yourself to move forward in a state of peacefulness.** You are letting go of the event, the person who harmed you, the hurt, the resentment. You are free!

Forgiveness does not mean that you have no boundaries and will let people run over you. It simply means that you are releasing yourself from the situation. It is a choice that we make. It takes us out of the "helpless victim" position and empowers us to have love and abundance in our relationships.

The issue of forgiveness is not just limited to our relationships with other people. We also have to learn to forgive ourselves. As I stated earlier, each of us is guilty of wrong behavior and hurting other people in some way, at some point in time.

When we fail, when we fall short, when we do something wrong in our relationships, I believe that our spirit holds us responsible and gives us the feeling of guilt. Guilt is a very powerful emotion. It makes us feel bad about ourselves and our actions. It tells us that we have done something wrong and calls us to make amends.

Unfortunately, most of us are uncomfortable to admit fault. As children, we tend to hide and lie when we do something wrong. As adults, we are often proud and arrogant. To admit fault or wrong doing is humbling and makes us feel embarrassed and vulnerable. So, most of us hide from our guilt and wrong doing.

If we hide from it, if we do not make amends, the energy attached to it will be stuck in our body and our unconscious. Over time, it will eat at us and punish us and compromise our ability to love ourselves and other people. We will become hostage to it and to our unexpressed wrong doing.

Admitting our wrong doing, seeking forgiveness and forgiving ourselves allows us to move forward. Our bodies and our spirits are returned to a state of peacefulness.

The Twelve-Step program is so successful in helping people recover from their addictions and their shattered lives because it incorporates these spiritual principles. When people are at peace inside themselves and in their relationships, the need for addictive substances is diminished.

The 4th step in the Twelve-Step program is to write a searching and fearless personal moral inventory. The 8th step is to make a list of all persons we had harmed. The 9th step is to make direct amends to such people, except when to do so would further injure them or others. Every marriage, every relationship needs these action steps. It is an on-going process.

To aid in your understanding of forgiveness, I will present some real life situations that show the impact of forgiveness.

FORGIVENESS IN CANCER PATIENTS

When I was an Oncology social worker working with cancer patients, I was curious to see that many of these people, deep inside themselves, were harboring resentments or hurt and a lack of forgiveness. Through training based on the cancer research of O. Carl Simonton, MD and Stephanie Matthews-Simonton, I learned that these strong, unresolved feelings were depressing their immune systems and might have made them susceptible to the development of cancer.

It was literally a matter of life and death for them to release these past hurts and concentrate all their resources on healing. If a cancer patient can begin the process of forgiving *Self* and others and take responsibility to change unhealthy parts of their lives soon after they are diagnosed, there is a high probability that healing will occur. This process can be enhanced by working with those trained in cancer counseling, by participating in Wellness Centers and by making themselves part of the treatment team — rather than letting the doctors make all the decisions. They must become proactive in their lives.

If the forgiveness work is not started until the patient is in the end stage of their fight against cancer, I have seen that those who forgive themselves and others have longer, higher quality lives, with less pain than those who remain bitter and immobilized.

FORGIVENESS FROM A CONCENTRATION CAMP SURVIVOR

My exploration of forgiveness continued when I read Corrie ten Boom's book, *The Hiding Place, 35th Anniversary Edition*. Corrie and her family were Dutch Christians who were sent to the German concentration camps for hiding Jews in their home and for participating in an underground network throughout Holland to save the lives of Jews. She lost her father, sister and nephew in the camps and narrowly escaped death herself. She had every right to hate the Nazis and cruel prison guards. And yet, after her miraculous release from Ravensbruck, due to a clerical error, God called her back to Germany, at the end of the war, to take the message of forgiveness to the German people.

The following direct quote from the book describes her own experience with forgiveness:

"It was at a church in Munich that I saw him, the former S.S. man who had stood guard...at Ravensbruck... He came up to me as the church was emptying, beaming and bowing. 'How grateful I am for your message, Fraulein,' he said. 'To think that, as you say, He has washed my sins away!'

"His hand was thrust out to shake mine. And I, who had preached so often to the people... the need to forgive, kept my hand at my side. Even as the angry, vengeful thoughts boiled through me, I saw the sin in them.... 'Lord...,' I prayed, 'forgive me and help me to forgive him.'

"I tried to smile, I struggled to raise my hand. I could not. I felt nothing, not the slightest spark of warmth or charity. And so again, I breathed a silent prayer, '...I cannot forgive him. Give Your forgiveness.'

"As I took his hand the most incredible thing happened. From my shoulder, along my arm and through my hand, a current seemed to pass from me to him, while in my heart sprang a love for this stranger that almost overwhelmed me."

I learned from these two experiences that the ability to forgive could be acquired and that we, in turn, are blessed and released when we forgive. It is an act of the Will, and God can help us if our Will is not sufficient.

FORGIVENESS IN MY OWN LIFE

In my personal life, I have experienced both sides of forgiveness. As a child, there were ways in which my parents harmed my emotional/psychological well-being. I had to learn to deal with the resulting wounds. I had to take responsibility to heal myself. I learned that I could not heal myself until I forgave my parents. Without forgiveness, I was uncomfortable in their presence, and I suffered from the hurt and resentment that were housed in my body. I longed to have a loving relationship with them, but I could not, until I forgave them. By not forgiving them, I kept myself in the role of "helpless victim" and was unable to establish intimacy with others.

I went through the process of forgiveness with both of my parents. When my father was dying, I had to decide whether or not I would go to see him. I was still very angry with him for being so indifferent to me throughout my life. "Why should I go to see him? He never came to see me." It took me days of struggle to make my decision. I knew deep down that I would regret not going to see him. It was my last chance. I also knew that as a therapist with experience dealing with death and dying, I had an obligation to help my father.

Soon after I got there, I realized that I had made the right decision. My father was dying and he was very afraid. He had been wandering in the hall, trying to escape the hospital. They had tied his wrists to the bed rails. Soon after I entered his room, I asked the nurses to untie him and said that he would be safe in my care. Over the next few hours, I was able to talk with my father, both as a wounded adult with wounded Inner Children, and as a therapist. I was able to ask my Daddy if he loved me

345

and hear his answer that he did. I was able to hug him and cry with him and feel at peace with him.

As a trained therapist, I was able to coach him about death and dying. "Are you afraid to die?" "Do you think there is life after death?" He said he was afraid. I told him I believed in life after death and believed he would be reunited with his loved ones who had passed on. I told him that he had the power to release his spirit from his body when he was ready. We talked about our life together and I kissed him goodbye. I received a call the next day telling me that he died peacefully in his sleep, and that he had not needed to be restrained in his bed. Forgiving my father was a blessing and a release for me.

I was also able to forgive my mother, many years before she died, and we experienced a wonderful last decade of her life. In forgiving her, I was able to give and receive the love and approval I had so desperately wanted from her. She, in turn, got to experience a relationship with a daughter who loved her, who was soft and appreciative in her presence. When she was 90 and I visited her in her assisted living apartment, she would say to me at night, "Do you want to spend over? You can." It was precious. We were two best friends.

Learning to forgive ourselves and others is a valuable skill that will enhance the quality of all our relationships. It is invaluable in a marriage. Each day in our roles as spouses and parents, we will be challenged in our ability to love one another. Some days we will be successful. Other days we will fail. Forgiveness is the skill which can help us balance our successes and failures.

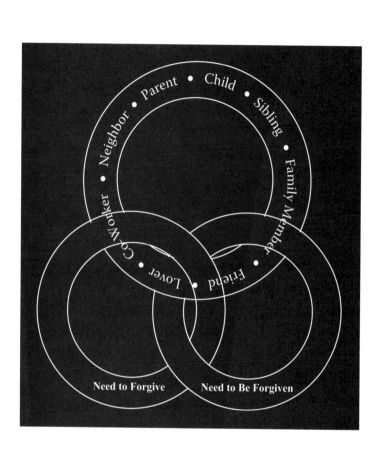

AFTERWORD

Reflections

Of all the flowers in God's creation, the rose is my favorite. A rose contains the paradox of beauty and thorns. A rose requires special handling and on-going maintenance. A rose can be attacked by pests, but is one of the hardiest of all plants. If it is properly nourished and maintained, the cost of the initial plant will reward you with years of beautiful, fragrant blossoms. A rose brings beauty and sensual pleasure to your eyes, your nose, your heart and your spirit. The branches of a healthy rose plant only strengthen and expand over time. Nothing can replace a mature rose plant in value and it is enjoyed and envied by all who come its way.

I envision each and every one of you, my Readers, as a rose plant. You were Divinely designed with inner beauty and potential. I hold you close to my heart and pray that you will plant yourself in the proper soil of knowledge and spiritual nutrients. I pray you will do the hard work necessary to find and maintain your *Self* and that you will find another beautiful rose plant to bring into your life. One rose plant is lovely, but two together make a beautiful garden.

It is my hope that my book will bless you on your life's journey and that the tools I have provided will help you maintain your growth for years to come. It has been an honor to come into your life.

APPENDICES

Section One

Direct Passages from Erik H. Erikson's *Childhood and Society,* Chapter 7, "Eight Ages of Man."

"In this book the emphasis is on the childhood stages...of the life cycle.... Psychosocial development proceeds by critical steps — "critical" being a series of turning points....Each critical item of psychosocial strength...is systematically related to all others, and...they all depend on the proper development in the proper sequence."

1. Basic Trust vs. Basic Mistrust

"...Mothers create a sense of trust in their children by that kind of administration which in its quality combines sensitive care of the baby's individual needs and a firm sense of personal trustworthiness within the trusted framework of their culture's life style. This forms the basis in the child for a sense of identity which will later combine a sense of being "all right," of being oneself....

The general state of trust, furthermore, implies not only that one has learned to rely on the sameness and continuity of the outer providers, but also that one may trust oneself."

2. Autonomy vs. Shame and Doubt

"...Outer control at this stage, must be firmly reassuring....As his environment encourages him to "stand on his own feet," it must protect him against meaningless or arbitrary experiences of shame and doubt....

From a sense of self-control without loss of self-esteem comes a lasting sense of good will and pride."

3. Initiative vs. Guilt

"...Initiative adds to autonomy the quality of under-taking, planning and "attacking" a task for the sake of being active and on the move....

He is eager and able to make things cooperatively, to combine with other children for the purpose of constructing and planning, and he is willing to profit from teachers....

The danger of this stage is a sense of guilt over the goals contemplated and the acts initiated in one's exuberant enjoyment of new locomotor and mental power."

4. Industry vs. Inferiority

"...He...becomes ready to apply himself to given skills and tasks....He develops a sense of industry....In all cultures, at this stage, children receive some systematic instruction....

The child's danger, at this stage, lies in a sense of inadequacy and inferiority. If he despairs of his...skills or his status among his...partners, he may be discouraged from identification with them....

This is socially a most decisive stage: since industry involves doing things beside and with others."

5. Identity vs. Role Confusion

"...in puberty and adolescence all sameness and continuities relied on earlier are more or less questioned again, because of a rapidity of body growth which equals that of early childhood and because of the new addition of genital maturity.

The growing and developing youths, faced with the physiological revolution within them, and with tangible adult tasks ahead of them are now primarily concerned with what they appear to be in the eyes of others as compared with what they feel they are...

The danger at this stage is role confusion...

Young people can also be remarkably clannish, and cruel in their exclusion of all those who are "different," in skin color or cultural background, in tastes and gifts, and often in such petty aspects of dress and gesture as have been temporarily selected as the signs of an in-grouper or out-grouper. It is important to understand (which does not mean condone or participate in) such intolerance as a defense against a sense of identity confusion."

6. Intimacy vs. Isolation

"...the young adult, emerging from the search for and the insistence on identity, is eager and willing to fuse his identity with that of others. He is ready for intimacy, that is, the capacity to commit himself to concrete affiliations and partnerships and to develop the ethical strength to abide by such commitments, even though they may call for significant sacrifices and compromises....

The avoidance of such experiences because of a fear of ego loss may lead to a deep sense of isolation and consequent self-absorption."

7. Generativity vs. Stagnation

"Generativity...is primarily the concern in establishing and guiding the next generation, although there are individuals who, through misfortune or because of special and genuine gifts in other directions, do not apply this drive to their own offspring. And indeed, the concept generativity is meant to include such more popular synonyms as productivity and creativity....

Generativity...is an essential stage...on the psychosocial schedule. Where such enrichment fails ... a sense of stagnation and personal impoverishment...early invalidism, physical or psychological, becomes the vehicle of self-concern."

8. Ego Integrity vs. Despair

"Only in him who in some way has taken care of things and people and has adapted himself to the triumphs and disappointments adherent to being, the originator of others or the generator of products and ideas — only in him may gradually ripen the fruit of these seven stages. I know no better word for it than ego integrity....

The lack or loss of this accrued ego integration is signified by fear of death....Despair expresses the feeling that the time is now short, too short for the attempt to start another life and to try alternate roads to integrity."

Section Eight

The Hiding Place, 35th Anniversary Edition by Corrie ten Boom with Elizabeth and John Serrill, (1971, 1984, 2006), Pages 247-248, Chosen Books, A Division of Baker Publishing Group, P.O. Box 6287, Grand Rapids, MI 49516-6287.

References and Other Reading Material

- *A Gentle Path Through The Twelve Steps,* by Patrick Carnes, Ph.D

- *Alcoholics Anonymous,* by Alcoholics Anonymous, New York, NY

- *Beyond Ourselves,* by Catherine Marshall

- *Childhood and Society,* by Erik H. Erikson

- *Daily Word*, by Silent Unity

- *Diagnostic and Statistical Manual of Mental Health Disorders,* Text Revision, Fourth Edition, American Psychiatric Association.

- *Dreams and Healing; A Succinct and Lively Interpretation of Dreams*, by John A. Sanford

- *Facing Codependence: What It Is, Where It Comes From, How It Sabotages Our Lives*, by Pia Mellody

- *Getting the Love You Want: A Guide for Couples*, by Harville Hendrix

- *Getting Well Again: The Best Selling Classic About the Simontons' Revolutionary Lifesaving Self-Awareness Techniques,* by O. Carl Simonton, M.D., Stephanie Matthews-Simonton, James L. Creighton

- *Hind's Feet On High Places,* by Hannah Hurnard

- *The Hiding Place,* 35th Anniversary Edition, by Corrie ten Boom

- *The Power of Intention: Learning to Co-Create Your World Your Way*, by Dr. Wayne Dyer
- *The Road Less Traveled*, by F. Scott Peck.
- *The Twelve Steps for Adult Children*, by Friends in Recovery
- *Women Who Run With the Wolves,* by Clarissa Pinkola Estes, Ph.D.

Art Work Featured in the Text, Printed in Full Color

**Sculpture that was made by a graduate art therapy student of mine
(Joyce Emmer, Graduate Program in Marital and Family
Therapy; Clinical Art Therapy, Loyola Marymount University,
Los Angeles, California)**

Annie

Charles Precious

Tomboy Judy

Judith Anne

Expanded Art Work

Heather

Heinrich #1

Heinrich #2

Heinrich #3

Heinrich #4

Heinrich #5

Heinrich #6

Heinrich #7

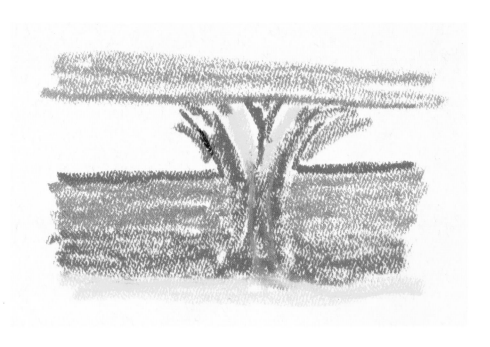

Heinrich #8

Heinrich #9

Heinrich #10

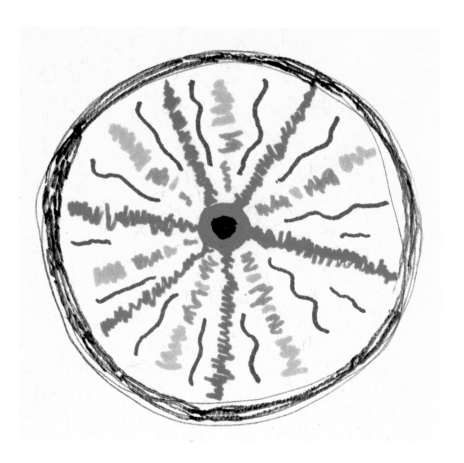

Heinrich #11

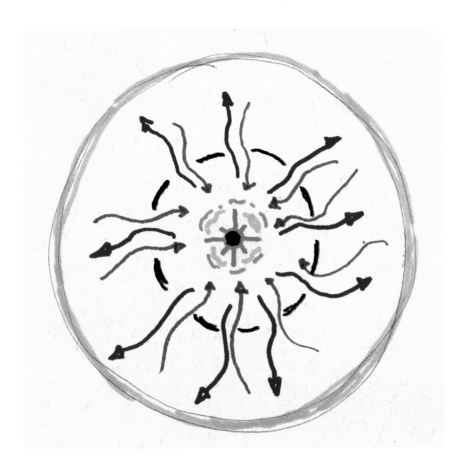

Heinrich #12

Heinrich #13

Index

U

W

Y

About the Author

With listings in *Who's Who in the World*, *Who's Who in America*, *Who's Who in Medicine and Healthcare*, and *Who's Who in American Women*, Judith has combined her own personal journey of healing and transformation with her holistic approach to treatment in this exciting book. As an educator, she has taught nationally and in Canada, and has maintained a thirty-three year holistic private psychotherapy practice.

Being raised in a military family and traveling extensively gave her an appreciation for all cultures and all the world's religions. She says her greatest achievement is her happy, healthy marriage and her relationships with her children, their spouses and her grandchildren.

She is a Licensed Clinical Social Worker, a Board Certified Diplomat in Clinical Social Work, and a Master Social Work Addictions Counselor.

Additional copies of
Creating a Healthy Life and Marriage
are available through your favorite
book dealer or from the publisher:

Spirit House Publishing
3435 Ocean Park Blvd.. #107-418,
Santa Monica, CA 90405
310-701-5481
Fax: 310-392-6281
Website: www.SpiritHousePub.com
E-mail: spirithousepub@verizon.net

Creating a Healthy Life and Marriage
(ISBN: 978-0-9843875-0-2)
is $28.95 for hardbound edition, plus
$5.50 shipping for first copy
($2.00 each additional copy)
and sales tax for CA orders.